The Girl Called
'Cigarette'
Never Quits

Renée DePeppe-DeMonaco

Book cover design by Gia DeMonaco

Published by: AJG Publishing

Contents

Dedication

To my grandmother, Dorothy Littell Forgage, the angel in the closet, who, I believe, watched over, protected, and guided me to my husband, Anthony, whose unwavering devotion to our marriage and family over the past thirty-two years enabled me to rewrite my narrative and make this memoir with purpose a reality.

Acknowledgments

Mom and Dad: Thank you for stopping at Gecker's Pharmacy on the way home from the hospital in November 1966 to buy a humidifier for me, always trying to raise me right with the help of Dr. Spock in the beginning. I know I was a wild card.

My children, Alex, Jake, and Gia; for the lessons you provided me through being your mother and raising you the best way I knew how.

New Jersey City University; for providing the bridge and supporting services enabling me to graduate college and rewrite my narrative.

Grand Canyon University; for providing me with the knowledge to analyze and understand my own reading journey.

My younger sisters, Dena and Noel; for finishing college years ahead of me, inspiring me to follow their lead.

For all the students I have worked with through the years, it has been a reciprocal relationship.

For all the friends made during my childhood and later on, coworkers turned friends, and family who took the time to laugh, talk, advise, provide a tissue when I needed one, teach me the pigeon stretch, share epically long phone conversations, text a TikTok to send a laugh, come into my class and give me a few minutes to catch my breath, walk at the Bayonne Hometown Fair or a chance meeting at the Bayonne Food Truck Festival, walk on the Asbury Park boardwalk followed with dinner at Pete and Elda's, spoke up for me as my Union Rep, had a quick lunch at Vinnie's on Danforth, Taco Bell, or DePalma's on Westside, shared family cruise vacations over the years, or time in Ocean City, MD years after a sketchy vacation in Wildwood, NJ, with your new baby. Whether we just shared a meal, coffee, or drink, you included me at a celebration or a get-together in your yard while taking your time to cook or order food, we attended a Broadway play after attending mass at Saint Patrick's Cathedral, or you donated resources to support my students, played Monopoly in your kitchen to recreate the old days, created holiday crafting and baking memories, came to a fundraising event I hosted, made pizza with me in my kitchen, gave or took advice, or we worked out past disagreements. I love you all.

Dana; for being the first person to read my book, being an on point fact checker and adviser, and finally, giving me the courage to press play.

Larry Gannon, I'll never forget your kindness.

About the Author

Renée was raised and has lived in Hudson County, NJ, for most of her life with her family and loyal pet and companion, Jessie. Renée has been a teacher in Jersey City, NJ, for the past 21 years. Over the years, Renée has worked as a cleaning girl, newspaper delivery person, laundry lady, men's formalwear professional, money transfer editor, mortgage department clerk, legal secretary, winery worker, bad diner waitress, cocktail waitress, hot dog cart and Italian ice vendor, food truck owner, restaurant owner, inventor, USPS mail carrier, and finally was "called" to be a teacher, most importantly, a special education teacher, reading specialist, and now an author. Renée also serves as a mentor who provides extracurricular activities to her mentees and is a high school bowling coach. Some of Renée's favorite things to do besides visiting with her grandchildren and staying in the loop with her nieces and nephews are walking Jessie, reading, quiet meditation, stretching, and a weekly infrared sauna. Other interests include being a neighborhood advocate and conducting a daily litter patrol. Renée enjoys short trips to Atlantic City with her husband and making pizza for her family on Friday nights while listening to freestyle classics from the early 80s with a Cosmo or glass of wine nearby, depending on her mood.

Foreword

Embracing Resilience and the Power Within

In a world that often tries to define us, one young girl stands tall, defying the odds and proving that the strength that resides within each of us is what defines us. In "The Girl Called Cigarette Never Quits," we are privileged to embark on a remarkable journey with a captivating protagonist who refuses to be overshadowed by adversity. At every turn, she reminds us that our spirit can soar beyond even the darkest of clouds.

From the moment we meet her, our hearts are pulled towards the enigmatic characters. Struggling to find her place in a world that constantly threatens to extinguish her light, she unveils a resilience that will leave an indelible mark on our souls. Through every trial, she never loses sight of her dreams, paving the way for us to discover the unyielding potential within our own lives. As the pages of this book unravel, we witness a spectrum of emotions that mirror the depths of our human experience. We feel the heartache of shattered dreams, the weight of discrimination, and the debilitating power of judgment. But the true genius of this book lies in its ability to seamlessly weave these moments with threads of hope, love, and unwavering determination.

Indeed, the author of this masterpiece, Renée DeMonaco, skillfully captures the intricacies and complexities of life, painting a vivid portrait of the world we inhabit. With her words as our guide, we accompany the author on her journey, confronting the harsh realities that often threaten to crush our spirits. Yet, it is through these challenges that she discovers her inner strength, revealing the grit and resilience that lie dormant within us all.

"The Girl Called Cigarette Never Quits" is not just a story; it's a testament to the human spirit—an anthem for those who refuse to succumb to the darkness that envelopes us. It reminds us that even the smallest flicker of hope can ignite a flame that brightens the path ahead.

As we turn the final page of this profoundly moving book, we are left with a profound sense of inspiration and empowerment. Renée's unwavering determination encourages us to confront our own battles and defy the limitations life often imposes. We realize that quitting is not an option, for our dreams, our aspirations, and our potential are far too valuable to be cast aside.

So, dear reader, open your heart and mind to this extraordinary tale. Allow Renée to take you by the hand and guide you through the maze of life's challenges. Embrace her triumphs, share in her sorrows, and let her unwavering spirit remind you that within each of us lies the power to soar.

"The Girl Called Cigarette Never Quits" is more than a book; it's a beacon of hope and an invitation to cultivate resilience within ourselves. May this story serve not only as a captivating read but also as a reminder that, even in the face of adversity, we possess the strength to overcome, the tenacity to endure, and the brilliance to light up the world.

-Lewis Spears

Author, Entrepreneur, & Educator

Chapter 1: Remember Where You Came From

Everyone has a backstory, and never forgetting where you came from is an important part of staying grounded and paying forward. Forgetting where you came from is something that really bothers me. My parents were the first generation in my family to own a house, a real fixer-upper back in 1970. It was an old, two-family home that needed to be brought back to life.

It had dark green asbestos shingles and no parking. My mom spent the first few years transforming this house on a very tight budget into a home for the family.   Mom was the original "design on a dime" housewife. My dad's mom, Grandma Jessie, lived downstairs from us. She had very bad rheumatoid arthritis, and making her weekly trek into the living room to watch the Lawrence Welk orchestra play on the TV was the highlight of her week once her arthritis really set in a few years after we moved in.

My parents were able to put together a down payment on the house with insurance money from my grandfather shortly after my Pop-Pop passed so that my grandmother could live on the first floor, and we lived upstairs. My very first memory is sitting on my Pop-Pop's lap in their apartment, an apartment I'd visit years later. I was three, and Pop-Pop was bouncing me on his knee in his chair. That's all I remember, but shortly after that, he passed away at work one day, waiting for his truck to be unloaded; just as he lit his pipe, he had a heart attack and died. I'm not sure how I found out that he was gone, but I remember being sad when I was told that he went to Heaven. I then became worried that my mom would pass away. My mother was pregnant with my sister, Dena, at the time and would nap on the couch in our 3rd-floor apartment. I would go over to the couch and open up her eyes or touch her face to make sure she was still alive.

Shortly after she had Dena, mom was standing over the crib and fainted backwards and fell on the floor, and was out for a bit. I'm not sure how long, but I was three and a half at this point, and I remember kneeling over her and worrying about how I was going to take care of the baby in the crib and thinking that she was dead. From a young age, I developed a habit of worrying about my mother because of my Pop-Pop disappearing suddenly from my life and being too young to understand that my mom was just pregnant and tired. She fainted because she just gave birth and was exhausted, but not dying. I can remember being obsessed with worrying about her not being there and how I would be able to take care of myself and my sister. These are my earliest memories.

I never knew my mom's parents, but she has told me about them for years. My Grandmother Dorothy, took care of other people's children and cleaned houses. My Grandfather Michael, worked on tugboats in the Hudson River. I come from a modest beginning. My dad was in the Army and, through the GI Bill, became the first person in the family, besides his younger brother,

Gerald, to go to college. Dad graduated when I was in first grade, about one year behind his brother, who is seven years younger. All my grandparents went to school no further than sixth grade.

My parents and the parents of my generation, in general, were not helicopter parents at all. Basically, I was told to go out and play all day in the summer, and my mom would throw push-up ice pops out the second-floor window to us. There were times when she'd even toss down a sandwich for lunch if she was mopping the floors and didn't want us to come in and walk over them. There was one time when my three-year-old sister, Noel, was brought back home by the police. She was spotted on the roof of the three-story apartment building next door with her friend. Today child services would have had to make a few visits to the house, but this was all very acceptable at the time, considering how my parents grew up in the late 1940's and 50's in Jersey City and Bayonne.

My mom still tells stories of her early youth, taking the bus to summer camp by herself at seven, and my dad as well. They would cross paths on the Boulevard bus, my dad going into Jersey City and my mom going to the pool at the city line between Bayonne and Jersey City. My mom grew up on Fairmount Avenue near McGinley Square and the Alps Restaurant. She graduated in the last half-year class from Lincoln High School in January of 1961. She often reminisces about growing up in Jersey City in the 1940's and 50's. The kids would gather from the neighborhood to walk to Lincoln Park, crossing the Boulevard, a busy four-lane thoroughfare, and then walking several blocks and crossing a few more streets. Sandwiches in brown bags, no plastic wrap or tinfoil, maybe just sugar and butter on bread. This posse of kids would range from tweens to three. The little ones would pile into old coach carriages that were much larger and deeper than what we see today. Possibly two or three kids were able to sit in the coach, and they would be off to Lincoln Park for the day with no parental supervision. Any adult in the area would guide them, and there was an understanding that any passing adult would have the right and authority to give the children instructions and advice.

My dad's mom, Grandma Jessie, had him driving a car at twelve, and when he resisted, she asked him, "Are you chicken?" She had a small fender bender and wanted my dad to bring the car to the auto body shop. My dad didn't want the responsibility of taking the car to the shop, but my grandmother had other plans. She was a real pistol. She once told a nun who was teaching my dad at Sunday school, "Do you know who my brother is? If you ever touch my son again, I'll have you rubbed out."

Grandma Jessie was raised by her aunt, and her brothers and sisters were actually her cousins. She was a "lovechild" born in 1914, which must have been a heavy load in those days. Her mother passed away when she was three years old, so her mother's sister raised her. Once my grandmother had her own family, she was extremely protective of her own family unit. She and my grandpa, Jake, dated but had broken up, and my grandmother was about to marry someone else. My grandpa was in the tavern right before the impending marriage and told my grandmother's brother that the only woman he ever loved was about to marry someone else. My grandmother's brother went home and told my grandma about his encounter with Jake at the bar and my grandmother went straight there and said to him, "I hear you still love me. Is that true?" I'm assuming my grandmother got the response she wanted and immediately broke off the wedding, which as family history recalls, was the next day.

After my grandfather had passed and my grandmother was living in her part of our two-family house, my grandmother and I would go for small grocery orders across the street to the A&P. I was five or six at this time. There was a produce man that would make small talk with my grandmother, and one day I said to her, "You should go on a date with him." She immediately slapped me very hard across my face and scolded me very harshly to never say that to her ever again. She emphatically told me she would never be with any other man but my grandfather. I ran home crying but understood my grandmother a little better, and I never did make any further suggestions.

My parents grew up completely differently than the kids of today are growing up. I was somewhere in the middle.

Dad told me about one time when he and his brother had a fistfight over bologna and salami, which were Christmas gifts. Yes, they each received whole, uncut deli logs of bologna and salami that they would measure at night before going to bed so they would know if someone ate any of their treasured deli meats. One day, my Uncle Gerald noticed that his bologna was shorter than he had remembered and, upon measuring, realized that some of his treasured meat was missing. He ran into the living room and jumped on my dad's back from behind. Dad was lying on his stomach on the floor with his hand under his chin, and the force of my uncle jumping on his back knocked out his two front teeth. This caused my dad to have some dental work that discolored through the years. I had asked him about his discolored tooth one time, and he told me this story of how it came to be.

Other stories about my dad include taking me to the Lyceum theater every couple of weeks to see the latest movie. We would walk fifteen blocks from our house. I saw "Rocky" with him and many other movies. We would talk on the way back and forth, and he would use this as a time to catch up with what I was up to in my life. Sometimes we would stop in for a slice at Palermo Pizza, across from the theater. My dad did his best to connect with me. I remember the last time we took that walk, I had already been dating my future husband Alex, and I told him I had tried cocaine. I remember how stiff he became, knowing how it feels to be a parent now. He most likely was scared shit; he was trying to act like I could tell him anything. My dad did his best, and I know he loved me.

My dad was a Capricorn, a man of his word. He would be calm most of the time, but when he exploded, you best get out of the way. One night when I was about fourteen, I was late getting home because I missed the bus. I was about half an hour late. It may have been nine-thirty, and I was due home by nine. I walked in the door, and he took me by my neck and lifted me off the floor, and pinned me against the wall. He was about two inches away from me, and his saliva was hitting my face as he was screaming. After a few seconds, I came back at him and sarcastically said, "Say it, don't spray it." Well, my father then took me from the wall of the kitchen and dragged me about eight feet over into the bathroom, and stuck my head in the toilet bowl! Yes, all this with my mother jumping on his back trying to stop him.

There was a time maybe two years before this when I was about twelve, and there was a single out, a forty-five record, as we would say, I'm talking about vinyl. It was a disco song that had a beat I really liked, and it was the first record I bought at a record shop downtown. I made a special trip on the bus to go get it. The song was "In the Bush" by Musique. The lyrics went, "Push push in the bush, you know you want to get down…" I brought this record home and played it over and over again on the family stereo. When my dad came home from his shift at the firehouse, he stopped and stiffened, listening to the lyrics, and went over to the stereo, which was a major piece of furniture in the house. He lifted up the lid to the stereo, removed the needle from the record, lifted up the record, and smashed it over his knee, shattering it into pieces. The whole time standing there in shock, now crying, and asking him why he did that, he was screaming and yelling at me, telling me never to bring such garbage and profanity into this house again. I'm totally confused because I'm twelve and literally think they're singing about pushing someone into a hedge. I'm telling my dad that's what the song is about and that he's wrong. He was so angry and just said, "That's not what the song is about, and that's it!" That was it.

Another incident at the dinner table was when I was about sixteen. I informed my parents that I planned to join the Army. My father went totally bananas. He had a vein in his neck that would pop out when he became very mad, his face would get red, and his eyes would bulge and become very intense. He started banging his fists on the table, saying, "No daughter of mine is going in the Army!" The spit was flying out of his mouth again, which I knew meant he was really hot, and you'd better clear the deck. He wasn't having it. Mom tried to talk to him and calm him down, but that wasn't an idea that he was getting behind. Considering that my mother had almost joined the Marines, I was shocked by this reaction. Mom had gone to a recruiting office and was in the process of joining the Marines but later was talked out of it by a guy she had met there while waiting to take her physical. She ended up dating that guy for a while before she met Dad.

When Dad was in the Army, he was thrown out of a diner down south in Georgia because his complexion was too dark. This really stuck with him. He was called racist names, and the whole group of guys left the diner with him that day because of this. He would tell us that story and be always hurt by it, and that may have helped him understand, a tiny bit, something about how People of Color feel at times.

He couldn't really understand, but he thought he did, in a small way, from what had happened to him. Whenever he had the opportunity, he would always tell us how "Italians" had been looked down on when he was a kid and were considered "less than" the Irish kids. He also believed that he was passed over for promotions at work because of his ethnicity and because he wasn't part of the good ol' boys of Bayonne. In his own way, he felt that he understood discrimination and had experienced it as well.

My father's heroes were Muhammad Ali and Joe Namath. His politics were moderate, but he was definitely an active member of the NRA. My dad was chauvinistic in his thoughts, but a man of his word. So much so that he didn't promise much because he didn't want to let you down. I grew up watching sports with my dad, football, boxing, wrestling, swimming, and playing dominoes. He played sports with different groups of friends all his life, including football in the schoolyard with the original Woodrow schoolyard crew into his late twenties. Then softball leagues up until just a few years before he passed. My dad really needed a son; he loved sports. He was on the football team in high school, but my Grandma Jessie battled both breast and lung cancer in her life. She was very sick when my dad was in high school, and he had to take over running the house. His brother, Gerald, was seven years younger and needed to be looked after during this time. My dad had to quit football, and the coach was very disappointed in him and told him he was a quitter. This bothered my father all his life, and because of that, he never quit anything he started, even school courses he didn't like. When he first went to college, his goal was to become a football coach, but he ended up with an accounting degree.

He took me hunting and to the gun range from the age of ten. I shot a gun for the first time at the range around eleven. Walking in the woods with him while wearing an orange vest as he hunted birds in the woodlands of New Jersey was a Saturday outing now and then. My dad loved football so much that when a game was on, our house would literally shake from his jumping and screaming. He was a Giants fan and, at times, a Jets fan too. He passed away the night of the Super Bowl in February 1999 when the Broncos defeated the Falcons. The team he was rooting for all season was knocked out of the playoffs by the Broncos, so when they won the Super Bowl, he was worked up, to say the least. He went to bed very upset, causing him to have a heart attack in his sleep as a result of congestive heart failure issues at only fifty-seven. He didn't smoke or drink. He lifted light weights several times each week to keep in shape. He liked to eat and was somewhat overweight. In his younger years, his nickname at the firehouse was "Garbage Can" because he would eat so much at fire department cookouts.

On Friday nights, he would sit in his house pants, which were karate pants or scrubs, and he would clean his rifles. The butt of the gun on the floor between his legs, he would be working the long brush up and down the barrel of the rifle. I didn't realize it then, being completely obtuse to his purposeful plans. He would sit there every weekend as different boys came and went from the house, working his brush, looking up at who came through, and nodding his head. He did this through all the years he had teenage girls.

These are the shoulders I stand on. I always try to remember that when I'm with my students in Jersey City. I always feel like I was one of them forty years ago, and my goal is to show them that I didn't forget where I came from. If I could make it, they could make it. That's the message I try to bring into my classroom every day.

I had worried about the same things they worry about, my parents, money, and asking my parents for things that they couldn't afford but I wanted. Some days when a student comes into my class, and I can see that there is something more on their mind, I go right back to when I was a kid worrying about something at home, and I automatically pause and say to myself, how would I have wanted my teacher to talk to me or to handle me, and that is exactly what I try to do every day I spend with my students. That's why I'll continue throughout this book to share events throughout my life that had meaning to me after reflection. I include some of the bad things that happened, but I'm not looking for sympathy. I am not a victim in any way. I have taken all my life experiences and applied them to my classroom for the past twenty-one years. I always try to use a moment that made me feel a certain way or a situation that I got myself into, and take the lesson and bring it forward to understand how someone else is feeling today in the here and now.

The trick is to harness your backstory and make it your focus for positive interactions going forward. Never regret an experience you have had. Own every experience you have gone through that you feel was a learning lesson for the positive or negative side of life. Every lesson has its purpose for your self-actualization. Once you see that, you will begin to look at your life differently. Take all the experiences that stand out, and the ones that you may have blocked out, and put them in your toolbox. Then use each memory to purposefully bring empathy and wisdom into all the interactions you have with other people. Empathy can change a negative into a positive moment for everyone involved. You can realize that something you experienced that you always perceived as a negative is really just part of becoming who you are now and enabling you to make the connections that you were put here to make. To help others by using your experiences, you can turn your negatives into positives, and help young people see their way through. The people that hurt or belittled you do not matter to this story. What matters is what they taught you.

A few years back, I had a student who had been having issues with OCD, and after talking with me, I referred them to the school psychologist. The student was immediately hospitalized because of an inclination to inflict self-harm. When the student was back in class, they wanted to talk to me about an ongoing struggle with repetitive motions that was making them very anxious about their recovery. I explained about a time when I was younger and was struggling with OCD as well. Every time I left the house, I was obsessed with worrying if I shut the flame on the stove burner off, worrying that the house would burn down. It was to the point that if I left for work without purposefully checking and noting it in my mind, I would need to go back home to check. I had to physically stop and see myself touching the handles and lock that into my mind before I could leave the house in peace each day. I told this student that if you are not trying to harm yourself or another, just go with it. Do what you need to do to feel you can keep going through your day. If it's touching a knob four times or tapping a chair before you leave the house, just do it with purpose. Once you take power away from the action and just go along, you will soon not need to do it anymore. This was advice from my own experiences, and I could see the lightbulb go off in their eyes. They smiled because they understood what I meant and felt it could work. That made my day because I remembered this difficult experience in my life and was able to use it to help this

16

student. I am always on a purposeful lookout to help someone with an experience I've had.

My husband's family has their roots in the Marion Projects of Jersey City. My father-in-law and his siblings grew up there and moved out when they were older teens into a rundown house on Arlington and Claremont Avenues. My father-in-law didn't hide that fact and was proud that by leaving school in the third grade and working, he was able to build a successful family business that supported his family. There is a family member of my husband's that was very vocal on Facebook during the Trump election campaign and was knocking people who are on public assistance. I called them out on Facebook, and we got into a back-and-forth, but what really stuck with me was that they had totally forgotten where their family came from, only one generation out. How can that be? I reminded this person that just as his family had benefited from public assistance programs and were helped up and out, they should support the same programs that could help others succeed in this country and move out of poverty. However, my words fell on deaf ears. Some people just don't get it. Agreed, you work hard and have made yourself successful but don't forget how you and the people whose shoulders you stand on got their chance to move up and out and get ahead, and acknowledge that your starting line was moved ahead a bit by that.

Being on the losing end was my narrative for most of my young life. I was put down, counted out, not taken seriously, insulted, made fun of, and overlooked. I took all these feelings of inadequacy, being shut out of mostly everything that I ever really wanted, and rewrote my narrative. I began to believe I was a loser because I was always treated like "less." Why? It all started because I was chubby as a little girl. I am a lefty and definitely think and process information and the world around me differently, always having difficulty following oral directions and learning to read. Definitely, a kid that would have had an IEP today, but during my childhood, that was almost unheard of. Because of all this, my teachers found me annoying and put me on the fringes from the very beginning. Sensing that vibe, I often fell out of my chair, asked the teacher to repeat the directions, maybe two times or more, and was often confused in school. It is what it is. My family had "less"; I had "less" than most of my peers in school as far as what kids deemed important.

I was an easy target because of all this. Kids can be cruel, and I cried a lot in my bed at night because of what went on at school. My parents were working with one income, so things were tight. Whatever it was, a negative narrative had been written and assimilated into my conscience about being worth less. There were mistakes made by my parents. All parents make mistakes, and my parents made their share with me, their firstborn and test dummy.

Chapter 2: Damaging Days

We would go to visit my mom's sister and her family a few times a year. It seemed we had a quarterly visit. We spent a summer day having a BBQ, and also visited for Thanksgiving, Christmas, and Easter during my younger years. They lived in the suburbs, and my aunt's husband was an executive for Revlon. They had a more refined lifestyle than we did, and it was a window for me to see where I would like my life to go. It's an important experience for a city kid to have an idea of what life outside of the city can look like. I was lucky to have that in my background. What I wasn't lucky to have was a male cousin, nine years older than me, who would molest me while my female cousin, eight years my senior, would stand by and watch, I surmise, to make sure no one came into the room. After they would touch me inappropriately, my cousin would give me a quarter not to tell. This surely didn't reinforce positive future sexuality and definitely caused me to be way too uptight for many years.

However, even this experience would provide me with empathy for what my daughter Gia would go through many years later and not react as a mother but as someone who understood.

When the kids were small, Gia was four, Jake six, and Alex fourteen, my husband Anthony's uncle found himself homeless. He came to live with us for about nine months. Mike lived downstairs in our vacant space, which was our restaurant that was now closed. I had just started teaching at this point, and we were busy. Mike would watch the kids for us sometimes when we went grocery shopping or to see a movie. One day we came back home from one of these trips, and as we walked in, Gia said, "Mike, tell Mommy the secret." A chill ran down my spine at that moment. Mike responded, "What secret? We don't have any secrets." and quickly went downstairs. I knew I needed to talk with Gia, but I wanted to keep things calm. Automatically my survival mode kicked in. Feeling frozen, I continued pushing through the moment but shut off emotionally to be able to function. This coping mechanism is what happens to me whenever I'm in extreme chaos or dealing with highly traumatic situations. This coping mechanism, gifted to me through my mom's grief, has served me well and given me a tool to use in situations with my own children and in my behavioral classes through the years.

I asked Gia to come and lie down on my bed with me, and I gently asked her to tell me the secret, reassuring her that she could tell me anything. When I heard what Gia had to say as she was crying in my arms because she was scared of what would happen next, I reassured her that she would never again see Uncle Mike during her entire life. I called my husband into the room and told Gia to tell her father what she told me. She was four at the time and said, "Uncle Mike kissed my butt." That was all we needed to hear.

My husband was in shock when he heard this and needed a few seconds to process it. I just said, "Get rid of him. I never want

Gia to see him again." I gave my husband very intense and serious eye contact, which told him not to speak another word or ask another question, but to just go do it right now.

Gia was very upset that she had to tell the secret she had promised to keep. He had been giving her gifts to keep the secret, and she felt like she had betrayed him. Gia was sobbing and very upset. As we lay there together, I was holding her and just trying my best to comfort her. What I remember the most is telling her how proud I was of her for telling me and how brave she was. I wanted her to know and feel that she did the right thing and not feel scared anymore. I asked her to describe what he did a few times to make sure that I understood exactly what had happened. My heart was broken and still will swell with that sinking, hollow feeling whenever I think about that day and what happened to our baby, and how Gia will always think about and deal with those memories. Thinking about my baby and based on my own experiences, I knew how heavily this would impact her psychologically. But I was also so proud of her for having the guts, at four years old, to say to Mike in front of me, "Tell Mommy the secret." She knew what he was doing was wrong and found a way to let me know so I could help her stop it. I thank GOD that she had that grit and bravery at that young age to fight back and save herself before things went even further. Knowing how Gia handled this gave me great confidence in her. I've always felt she'd be able to do anything she put her mind to. She knew she could tell me and that I'd make it all stop and go away. I was older when this happened to me and wasn't brave enough to tell.

Again, my own past experiences helped me to understand how Gia was feeling and to act in a way that I thought would be the best going forward. It was important to Gia to know that she would never face him again after she told us, and we kept that promise. He never was seen around our house or neighborhood ever again after that day. Anthony told everyone in his father's family, Mike's family, and anyone who Mike might go to for help, what he had done. He was banished and cast out. My older son Alex and his friends, all about fourteen at the time, found Mike one night soon after, squatting in an abandoned house in the area, and showed him just how much we all never wanted to see him again. We never did. His son came by one day and told Anthony that Mike ended up dying while hoboing on the trains in Pennsylvania.

Gia still struggles with this today and has therapy to work through leftover issues from being violated in that way. Honestly, I regret that I didn't put Gia into some type of therapy at that time, maybe art therapy, to work through what happened. She was in many different art classes through the years but not purposefully therapeutic. I was scared to tell anybody about what had happened because I didn't want her to be interviewed by Child Services and possibly taken away. I would try to check in with her about it, bring it up gently now and then, and ask her if she wanted to talk to me or someone about it, but she always told me she didn't want to.

I think when you have been through something like this, having someone stick up for you and tell you it wasn't your fault is very healing. For me, that came when I was dating a guy named Nick. I told him about my cousins and what they had done to me. I hadn't told anyone before. Then, sometime later, we went to my aunt's house for dinner, and Nick took a quarter out of his pocket, flipped it off his thumb to my cousin, and said, "Here's your quarter back. Renée told me." I couldn't believe he did that at the moment, but I was glad he did. It gave me a feeling of being validated and heard, and somehow, I was finally able to put it behind me after that. Knowing that my cousin was embarrassed helped too.

Gia never got that chance to know Mike was embarrassed or see him squirm because she was so young. I hope knowing what her Dad, brother, and everyone else in the family did behind the scenes to make him squirm, helps today.

I've had students share stories of extreme abuse while in sharing circles. Having had these kinds of experiences in my own home helped me with a few students through the years. It's important to know how to react and what to say to help a student who is sharing something that happened to them in the past, something that already had them removed from their home, but wanted to share, get it off their chest, and talk about their feelings in a less clinical setting. Having these experiences from my youth and being with Gia when she was able to tell me what was happening to her helped me to be the kind of listener these students needed at that moment. My point is that even these atrocious events added something to my war chest.

I always wondered why so many different taboo topics have collided in my life. After deep reflection over many decades, the only conclusion I can surmise is that it is so that I can share these experiences and help people see their way through the mistreatment and feelings of discontent, being misunderstood, undervalued, overlooked, and ignored. To understand that they also can rewrite their narrative from what others want them to be to what they believe they can be.

Chapter 3: Self-Efficacy Shifting

By middle school, I was already starting to get a chip on my shoulder and becoming more of a wise mouth. I was coming to a point in my mind where I had to start defending myself. I made friends with a girl who was tougher, and she taught me how to be more assertive about myself. We were friends for a while, but she was becoming too controlling and didn't want me to be friends with any of the other girls in school. She actually forbade me. With me, if you say I can't, I must. After that, we went our own ways after being friends for most of the seventh grade. The biggest thing I remember about her was that she had a Doberman Pinscher, and that dog would let me in the house to visit nice and easy, but when it was time to leave, I had to run for my life while her brothers held the dog back from biting off my leg.

Basically, I started to rewrite my narrative in my head in my early twenties but didn't take action until my early thirties. When my younger sister, Noel, graduated college, I realized that I could finish as well. She inspired me to get going. I changed my narrative from what people said about me to what I said about myself.

Apathetic and sarcastic teachers, misguided guidance counselors, unkind classmates, and people who at one time I considered my friends, said and asked outrageous things of me. I felt and believed that the adults around me, in school and even socially, did not see my true potential. There was always an inferred assumption that felt as if I wasn't good enough, or didn't have the potential, to be successful.

It could have been from being in the "B" class in grammar school. There were two homerooms for each grade. One class had all the kids who didn't really need a teacher. They could teach themselves. Give them a book, and they were good to go. They would read it and know all the material. In the other class, my class, the kids needed to be guided or wrangled in at times, requiring a teacher with more chops and a lighter delivery, all at the same time.

Being written off too quickly as just the girl who smoked cigarettes and wasn't as worthy were the vibes I felt being projected toward me in my childhood and early teens. All I really wanted was to be accepted as having the same possibilities, equal, and just as smart. I have always been an intuitive person and was sensing what was being projected toward me by the adults and kids who I was coming in contact with when I wasn't home. What I needed to understand was that what other people thought of me, my family, and my circumstances, didn't matter one iota. What mattered was what I believed I could do.

There were teachers who didn't include me in school plays. In fifth grade, I tried out for almost every part, if not every part, of "Annie," the school play being performed at Woodrow Wilson School. Raising self-esteem and an interest in theater wasn't part of the Playbill. My mother went to my school and gave Mrs.

Russell a firm tongue-lashing in my defense. My mother was always my biggest advocate, but she would also get very emotional and upset when people hurt me, so I hid a lot of my pain from her.

I was a fringe student because being part of the main players was never where I found myself throughout my life. Always someone on the outside looking in. My eighth grade teacher, Mr. Esposito, began calling me "Cigarette" in class because I was already smoking outside of school – effectively establishing my nickname for years to come. This nickname went so deep that my younger sister, Dena, was known around our neighborhood as "Little Cigarette." My favorite jeans at the time had cigarettes with billowing smoke rings pursed in red lips embroidered onto the back pockets, so it's fair to say I had acclimated to the nickname. Mr. Esposito used every opportunity to embarrass me among my classmates, when what he should have done was pull me aside quietly and try to have a meaningful one-on-one conversation with me. In another instance, a high school guidance counselor sat me down and told me I wasn't college material. I believed him.

These were the messages I was receiving during my impressionable early teenage years when my mind was forming its narrative about who I would be one day. The narrative I was writing wasn't very ambitious because the messages being received told me that I wasn't going to amount to much.

This tapestry, the one I've created in my mind, will weave together the various facets of my journey to self-actualization. To share my experiences and how I've come to realize that GOD had a plan for me from the very beginning and even before. My goal is to use all my life's experiences to bring hope and acceptance to people who may feel like there is no way past their present situation.

I've had the opportunity to confront many taboo issues and learn from them and develop true empathy in a wide range of situations. This is the journey I was meant to take all along, and the many difficult circumstances I've personally faced were all for a grander reason, to help other people see their way through a rough patch or difficult time. To be there with an empathetic ear and eye, to communicate that I've been there in an authentic way and that they are seen and understood. The reason for this compilation of experiences was to acquire a war chest of empathy to be able to be relatable and to help the students and other people I would meet throughout the many windows of my life and be able to touch them in an authentic way.

There was a time when I felt embarrassed by my life, but I have come to realize this was the path that was made for me to become the person I am today. This life and how it rolled out for me made me a very uniquely nuanced, empathetic, and intuitive person. My story is for people who need something to believe in. It's a true life story about making it through a tough childhood, rocky adolescence, turmoil-filled twenties, making mistake after mistake, choosing the wrong people to have faith in, and somehow beating the odds and making it through. I want to tell my story to the counted-out people. These are my people. I want this group to know that with faith and some hard work, you can accomplish anything you want to. What holds people back is negativity, a vibe, a feeling that projects from the people around them. To succeed in this life, you must have grit and be brave enough to risk a fall. If you can be brave and humble enough to admit that you need help and that you don't know everything, coupled with seeking help in the right places, asking someone to help you, asking GOD to help you, and combine that with being willing to take a chance, put yourself out there, raise your hand and ask a question, you can do what you were put here to do. Everyone has something to bring to this table of life, as long as you always keep two things in mind. Do not ever forget where you came from and the experiences that made you who you are, and most importantly, know that you can change a life just by being kind, and all that you want to do will come to you. You can rewrite your narrative and be who you want to be, not who other people say you are.

Just be kind, with purpose, and always try your best to leave each person better off than you found them. Make it a point to do that every day, all the time. A piece of gum, cookie, upbeat greeting, or small compliment left over from yesterday's class. Be positive in your perspective and bring that to all the people you come in contact with. This positive karma will multiply and come back to you exponentially, but you have to believe.

Unkind people kept me from my true potential for too long. One day I finally realized that what unkind people thought of me didn't matter to me anymore. What mattered to me was what I knew about myself. I had to sit down and really look inside myself, take the time to get to know who I am and what I really wanted to do with my life. After reflecting on this for many years, it dawned on me that this was what I was supposed to do with my life. All these toxic relationships and experiences in my background were all there for a reason. You have to come to terms with your past experiences. Even when these transgressions are embarrassing, you are the sum of these experiences, and they are yours to use to your benefit and to the benefit of others.

Turn your negative experiences into positives by using them as a tool to help yourself and others to not make the same mistakes or to not repeat them yourself. True empathy is wisdom, and wisdom doesn't come cheap. It is paid for with a high price – your emotions, dignity, humility, heart, and soul. So make your experiences count, even the ones that make you wince when you think about what you have done, where you have been, and what you said. Just flip it! Turn it on its head, and know you went through that for a reason. Probably to gain knowledge that will help someone through something similar someday down the road. To have the ability to look a person in the eye and let them know that you understand and have been there. That, right there, can change a life. This realization – coming to accept your life, your actions and mistakes, other people's actions and mistakes, and how all these experiences influenced you. This will empower and enable you to take hold of your life.

Take time to reflect on your life, cry, pray, meditate, contemplate, repent in your heart, release the things you have done that make you cringe, and release the resentment and grudges you hold against the people who have hurt you or held you back. Accept and acknowledge that all these things have made you the person you are today, both positive and negative. Take your toolbox of experiences on the road with you, and whenever someone comes into your focus, use your experiences to guide your actions. Say to yourself, "What did I really want or need someone to do for me when I was in this similar situation?" and do just that for them. This action will change your life and the way you look at the sum of all your life experiences, the good, the bad, and the ugly. This is what I believe I must share with my kindred spirits, the readers of this book. All the experiences I've had couldn't be insignificant in my life's journey. Living this life, the one I've been given has delivered to me a treasure trove of stories and experiences that have given me the gift of empathy and compassion for so many people and many different situations. This journey of mine is a result of following my heart through my life and not always using my head.

Chapter 4: What Was Less Worthy About Me?

I'll start somewhere in the middle…Reading to Alex as a toddler, I realized I needed to improve, and this is how it went from there…While standing in line at the checkout after grocery shopping when Alex was a baby, he would reach for the "Golden Books" in the kiosk, before there were kiosks, in a spinning display near the registers. Every week I would buy him the book that he grabbed. We would go home, and I would read these books to him, but at times I felt that my reading wasn't as smooth or fluent as it should be reading these very basic readers aloud to Alex. It was choppy and stilted. These books were the beginning of my journey to becoming a reading specialist. As is said, "It all starts with the first step," and for me, those Golden Books were the first step. I hadn't taken an interest in reading up to this point. I was literate and always could get my thoughts down on paper, but sustained reading just wasn't something that I had done up to this point. Honestly, I never had a book I was interested in. Fictional stories where you had to follow a plot were hard for me, but non-fiction, I could try. Part of that had to do with my guidance counselor putting me in commercial secretarial courses in high school, where I learned to take steno, type, and do accounting work. According to Mr. Morrish, I wasn't college material, and as I said, I believed him. I'll always remember sitting there with him, his eyebrows hanging down over his eyes as if they were curtains.

He had hair growing out of his nose and very heavy black-framed glasses. In his gravely, deep rough voice, he said the words that would seal my fate for the next fifteen years, "Miss DePeppe, you are not college material." Having that core grit, even then, I asked, "Why do you say that, Mr. Morrish?" He told me that I had taken some tests, and they revealed that I didn't have the aptitude for college. That was the explanation I accepted, and I went on to enroll in "business courses" in my sophomore year at Bayonne High School in 1981.

I went home and told my parents that I chose this course. I was too embarrassed to tell them what the guidance counselor had told me. So, I learned to type, take steno, and do bookkeeping work. These skills have served me well. I was able to find employment after high school and was capable of supporting myself and my son, Alex when we found ourselves on our own.

However, that clearly was not the track for me. After much contemplation, I came to understand that it must have been GOD's plan, because when I came to that fork in the road, I went down the road of the life of hard knocks for almost two decades. Yet I was able to build up a war chest of life experiences that served me well as a mother, special education teacher, and a reading specialist.

The first book I ever read cover to cover – besides children's books – was *A Child Called "It"* by Dave Pelzer. I built up to reading this book at about thirty years old. I had been reading

Golden Books to Alex for years and moving into reading children's books with him, and over about ten years, I slowly built up my sustained reading speed and ability to break down unknown words using syllables. The problem has always been that I have dyslexia, which went unattended to. I self-diagnosed during and after my years of training as a reading specialist. To this day, I have difficulty pronouncing certain words and breaking down unknown multisyllabic words. I know the procedure, but when I attempt to pronounce these words, I usually stumble. Auditory input, or hearing the word said correctly first, will help most of the time.

These persistent difficulties – after all my years reading complex texts – led me to understand that dyslexia had been part of my reading difficulties. This was the cause of my stumbling when reading aloud. So much of my working memory was being used on decoding, that my comprehension suffered. In grammar school, this was a factor that caused teachers to think I was less intelligent.

My written expressive language skills have always been better than my receptive and expressive reading skills. In college, I learned through writing the notes from class over, maybe twice, for neatness. Over the years, I have observed that students who shifted to less tactile input and who do not physically write notes throughout the educational process, struggle with memorizing important information. My students write and annotate, create illustrations, organize information in charts, complete exit tickets on index cards or Post-it notes, etc. – with pen or pencil and paper as much as possible – through high school. The kinesthetic act of actually writing helps process information into long-term memory. The loss of pen to paper in the classroom has limited some students. Blending phonemes together while writing spelling and vocabulary words in cursive helps many students who are kinesthetic learners. Scratch-Art paper to support students in learning multiplication tables is a powerful tool. This is a kinesthetic activity that will assist in hard-to-remember facts being processed because of the need to press hard to scratch out important content. The pressing causes deeper focus and assists in firing the synapses that will transfer the information from short- to long-term memory. Computers and keyboarding have their place, but do not supply the same intensity in the fingertips as pressing on a pen or pencil that scratches out the important content. When considering the fact that more memory input is processed through the nerves of the fingertips than through all other senses combined, it makes sense.

I would stumble when reading aloud, but when writing, if I wasn't on the spot completing a timed test, I usually did better. Anxiety was a problem for me from very young. This translated into poor self-esteem, and ultimately a negative self-narrative was internalized.

Being clumsy and chubby as a little girl caused me to always be picked last for teams in gym class. This was another time when I could remember just feeling awful and embarrassed. Knowing it was gym day would cause me anxiety before going to school. Often feeling like I just wanted to cry and hated my life when the kids would argue over who had to have me on their kickball or dodgeball team in the schoolyard. This didn't add anything positive to my developing narrative. After a few years, I made friends with some of the girls and was part of the Woodrow Schoolyard crew. We put together a softball team which our friend Candace's parents sponsored, so we were known as "Larry's Market." I was the catcher, and my friend, Debbie, a natural athlete, was the pitcher. Whenever a ball was thrown to home plate, when there were players on second or third, Debbie would run in and make sure I didn't mess up the play. These are the types of experiences that prevented me from developing a more positive self-image and negatively impacted my self-esteem. This wasn't Debbie's fault at all. It was just that my reputation for being poor in athletics was at a point that it predetermined my role – as other things in my life were predetermined – from what people "thought" of me and what I was capable of. These memories came rushing back when I started coaching bowling for Ferris High School. This past year was an amazing experience for me, and as always, I was able to take the experiences from my past to help right the wrongs – reinforcing that all these experiences were for something. I always try to make each member of my team feel positive about their ability – finding something to praise and giving a simple, gentle push after the praise. I always think to myself, "Remember how you felt when somebody didn't believe in your ability." Even though I was upset back then, I took those memories and flipped them on their heads, and made sure positive outcomes grew from them.

As teachers, parents, or other adults who stand to influence the lives of younger people, we need to keep in mind that we are shaping who our students believe they can be by building their self-esteem each and every day. It is not just the content curriculum we are teaching; we are also building up the child and, most importantly, their confidence in themselves. If we do this well, their self-esteem and self-efficacy will support them when things get tough. We have to show kids that they can take a risk and that making mistakes and needing practice are needed parts of growing.

This example may seem strange to most, but as a special education teacher, coats can be a huge issue in the classroom. Coats can make or break a school day for students with emotional or behavioral disabilities. It seems bizarre, but it's true. Some kids need security, and the heaviness that a coat or layers of hoodies bring to a student may be what they need to manage their anxiety and feel secure. As a special education teacher, I understand this. As a special education person, I know this. Sleeping is impossible for me without a heavy blanket over me. It makes me feel safe and secure. For twenty years, I've tried to explain to administrators, when they come into my classroom and demand that students take off their jackets and coats, that this is something that helps my students feel centered and secure. Please stop starting off the school day with demands of compliance that do not support a positive educational outcome, particularly in behavioral classes. It is very difficult to bring students back from a day that starts off with negative demands. The most critical and impactful part of the school day is the greeting in the morning and the blastoff, if you will. If you are trying to make a student give up their only layer of security as soon as they come in, you are setting their day up for failure – not to mention the impact that action has on their classmates... and the teacher. Think about how your own blanket makes you feel, or your beloved vest or blazer that provides the form to your outfit that gives you confidence.

Try to apply that to a kid in a classroom that wants to have that same security. As a teacher, I had often resented having to take valuable time out of my day to cajole a student into taking off their coat because the administration was pushing down on me – especially when I knew exactly why the student needed it. Is it really important that all students remove their coats in school, or is it just that the school needs to show that they hold ultimate authority? Not all students respond well to that type of confrontation. Students with emotional and behavioral issues, in particular, are set off by these nonsensical rules.

Chapter 5: Claiming Myself as Important

High school was much better than grammar school, but it still had its ups and downs. Rewriting my narrative was my goal at this time. Grammar school was probably the toughest part of my life because I felt powerless to do anything to change my circumstances, truly feeling like a victim. While I continued to battle with my self-esteem, I started to take control in high school by pushing myself – drawing a line in the sand that no one could cross.

I had a group of friends that I felt were my chosen family and a boyfriend that, at the time, I truly loved. We met in orchestra class at Woodrow Wilson School when I was in sixth grade, and Michael was in eighth. I played the clarinet and he played drums. While he was friendly to me, our "romance" had not yet begun because I was so much younger. I remember a time in the school hallway when Michael gave me a pep talk about kids making fun of me. He told me to ignore them and that they were just immature. I liked him automatically because he was kind.

Fast forward three years… Michael and I started "going out" when I was in eighth grade and he was a sophomore at Marist High School. Early in our relationship, he brought me to his family's apartment.. I recall feeling like it was very familiar, and I recognized the rooms and layout. Sure enough, my dad confirmed it was the same address and the same apartment where my dad and uncle brawled over logs of bologna and salami, and my Pop-Pop had bounced me on his knee. It was serendipity.

Michael and I had some amazing experiences together, which convinced me we were destined to be together. For starters, one night, we were sitting on my front porch discussing a problem and we were praying together. It was winter, maybe February, and it was very cold outside. To the left of my porch were three rose bushes that were dormant for the winter. As we were praying, the rose bush to the near left of us bloomed a pink rose right in front of our eyes.

This blooming rose was an amazing moment in my life, and I'd bet it is still an important moment for Michael as well. In addition to the rose blooming, as he was saying a prayer, the wind was picking up, and as he spoke louder, the wind became stronger, and when he went silent, the wind would become still. It was a very miraculous and mystifying night. We were both truly amazed and felt that our prayers would be answered and that this was a sign from GOD. We showed my mom the rose, but she didn't know what to say or do with it. I'm not sure she even believed us. Michael's mother brought it to the St. Vincent's Church rectory, but nothing ever came of it – except that the experience made me believe I was supposed to be with him, and it helped keep that flame burning for many years past what would be considered psychologically healthy.

I think our prayer that night had to do with one of our friends not finding out what we had said about them when we were talking privately on 57th Street. That's where we'd hang out all the time and talk about the small-scale politics and alliances of our friend group as Michael tried to get to "first base" for over a year. One of his "friends" had been recording us with a cassette recorder behind the door where we were talking about how we really felt about one of our friends. Honestly, nonsense, but also the beginning of me recognizing the depths that his friends would go to make sure we didn't stay together for the long haul. Jealousy and frightened of a relationship they didn't yet understand, were likely two things that had some of his friends acting like jackals.

One day I was walking through the schoolyard where our group would congregate. No one was around except for a group of five or six guys that were part of our "schoolyard crew." They proceeded to chase me and pushed me down on my stomach on the schoolyard asphalt. They were pulling at my underwear, saying they were going to give me a "wedgie." It was very scary and frightening for me. A few of them were yelling, "Do it, do it," as they grabbed at my pants. I was really frightened, screaming hysterically. When I look back at this, in my mind's eye, it was really a terrible case of bullying – which touched on sexual assault and intimidation – because I truly felt compromised. Guys usually give guys wedgies, not girls. Having these guys push me, hold me down by my shoulders, and grab at my pants was extremely traumatic. As I was screaming, another neighborhood guy, Larry

Gannon, heard me screaming for help as he walked up the block. Larry was a little older than us and had a reputation for being tough. He started walking really fast and then started sprinting toward the scene, yelling at the group to get off and away from me. Larry then began to physically push them away from me, screaming and cursing because of what he saw they were doing to me. They finally stopped and ran off. Larry saved my dignity and taught me that there are kind people who may come to you in disguise – their angel wings may just be concealed. Larry was a tough person who had a reputation as someone you'd be a fool to mess with. He showed me that day that what people say about you is really bullshit. Actions speak louder than words every day of the week. He wasn't a clean-cut Catholic schoolboy, but he was a goodhearted person. Larry helped me up and talked with me for a while until I calmed down. Once he made sure I was alright, he walked me part of the way home until he knew I was safe. I'll always remember the kindness he showed me that day. He was a hero in my eyes. I've always felt he saved me from a bad situation that could have gone too far because of the mob mentality vibe that was pervading the situation. Those boys weren't really thinking of what they were doing at that point; they were participating as a group, so there wasn't one who was to blame. It was a group activity, and it just kept going, and I'm not sure where that would have gone if Larry didn't come by and saved my ass, literally.

Many years later, when I told my husband, Anthony, about this experience, he said he knew Larry and that he used to hang out downtown where my husband grew up. Anthony recalls Larry as a guy who would always look out for the underdog or the weaker person. He was someone who would do the right thing and help when someone was outgunned. Anthony also told me about a friend of Larry's named Arthur – they were both into playing guitars and rock music. Arthur wasn't tough like Larry, and was bad in sports like me, but Larry remained friends with Arthur and always looked out for him to make sure people didn't take advantage of him. Larry is an angel in this world and was the first person to teach me to never judge a book by its cover.

After that day, I stopped going by the schoolyard and distanced myself from the "crew." When my very best lifelong friend, Dana, would have parties for the schoolyard crew, I would go. But I really didn't want to because I didn't enjoy being with those people. This is when I started to develop social anxiety – dreading to go to social events where I'd have to interact with people who were not in my inner circle. I was hanging out less with this group. It was always uncomfortable for me after that day in the schoolyard. Seeing my old boyfriend was difficult and I didn't want to be around his group of friends. I didn't consider them my friends – even though the other girls in the group did – and that became an issue for me. Some of the boys did other inappropriate things where I found myself in a vulnerable position, which cemented my feeling that these guys were far from gentlemen... or friends.

The Woodrow crew was a large group – more than forty when everyone was out. There were a lot of really memorable times before all this happened. There was always a big boom box playing all types of music in the schoolyard. It was the days of Sugar Hill Gang's original "Rapper's Delight." We would all sing the lyrics, word for word, while watching the guys play basketball during the day and drink Budweiser nips and peppermint schnapps at night.

When we were looking for a diversion, we would walk a few blocks, and with much assistance, I would hop the tall fence, and "party" behind Marist High School. On other nights, we would congregate under the NJ Turnpike overpass between Bayonne and Jersey City, or walk down behind the Hi-Hat catering hall and hang out by Newark Bay. I never liked going there because to get to the shoreline, we had to walk through very dense tallgrass filled with opossums.

One night a whole crew of kids from Prospect Avenue came up to fight the Woodrow crew. During the brawl, Larry, my hero, literally bit someone's earlobe off defending his Woodrow friends. Upon hearing about the impending brawl, I remember sliding down the steep concrete slab under the Turnpike overpass on my backside to go see what was happening. I was wearing my favorite jeans – which had embroidered red lips and a cigarette with smoke billowing up on the pockets – and someone yelled to me, "Hey, Cigarette." I didn't mind the name at that time. After all, those jeans inspired the jacket for this book.

There were plenty of good times, and a lot of really good people were part of the Woodrow crew. Five bad eggs out of forty or so is only eight percent, which seems about average. However, this really isn't about all that, so I will stop there.

Chapter 6: Starting the Rough Draft

Vinnie was a person who came in and out of my life for a short time. I always felt like I treated him wrongly, and karma came around and kicked me in the ass for it. This was a time when I was hanging out more with my friend Debbie, and I was away from the schoolyard most of the time. Our boyfriends were friends, so we were spending more time together as a foursome. We went to the Junior Prom together and things were pretty good.

My friendship with Candace was cooling off at the time. I think it had a lot to do with the fact that we were all stretching our wings. Michelle was with her boyfriend Charlie most of the time, and Jill, my first best friend, was dating Frank. It seemed we were scattering to the winds a bit. Kathy and I grew up on the same block, just up and across the street, yet we didn't connect much in high school. Through Dana, we became closer through the years when just "the girls" would get together. Kathy gave Gia my favorite baby dress ever, and I keep a picture of her in it on the back of my phone to this day. You know how it goes. For the first child, there is a baby shower. For the second baby, a few gifts, or a "sprinkle." For the third baby, gifts are few and far between, so it meant a lot to me.

Dana and I weren't really connecting overly at this time, but we always had a very strong bond since we became friends in third grade. We became friends through Jill, who was my best friend in third and fourth grade. The three of us had so much fun playing

Monopoly around the clock; we would have the same game going for days, and would just leave it in Jill's bedroom or, in the summer, put it aside on my porch when it was time to go home and continue the game the next day. The three of us were very serious – even ruthless – about Monopoly. I often think playing that game gave me the bug to want to own more than one house – something I haven't *yet* achieved. We also put on plays in my backyard for the younger kids on my block, making costumes and just being little girls together.

Jill is Jewish. I remember my father telling me to never tell Jill's family that my mom's family has German ancestry. Even after learning about American history, I'm not sure why my dad was worried about Jill's family being leery of my German heritage. If they were, they surely would not have been alright with my dad being one hundred percent Italian. Anyway, I'm sure Jill's family knew that my family and I had nothing to do with the atrocities of the Holocaust, but it's something that has always made me shake my head at my dad's thought process.

From a young age, I always had the travel bug in me that longed to explore the world and visit more exotic places than just Montauk and the Jersey Shore. I guess that's why I made up a wild tale and told Jill my family was going to Hawaii on vacation. I even sent her a postcard "from Hawaii," not knowing the postmark would have me made. When I "returned from vacation," Jill's mom asked how my trip was and how the plane was. I told her we drove there over a bridge. She never called me out on it or made me feel embarrassed about my lie. She just went along with me. She has always been a very nice woman. Both Dana and Jill had working mothers who did a lot. They were my first role models of working women who were away from home for many hours and had to come home and get it all done too.

It was influential for me to see that women could "do it all" and observe firsthand what a working woman would or should be. My mother didn't work outside our home during my childhood. She went back to work around the time I left home at eighteen, so I don't remember her as a working woman – though she did work for about ten years when I was older. Once grandchildren started arriving on the scene, she was very involved in covering holes in childcare for all six of her grandchildren.

She watched Alex a few days a week for me when he was small. I remember her calling me at work in downtown Manhattan at 4:55 p.m. When I'd answer the phone, she'd say, "You're still there!?" I'd respond, "Ma, I work nine to five, it's not five yet!" Alex would run her ragged, but she was still young in those days, and I know she and my dad enjoyed him very much.

Growing up, the women who were part of my life outside my house gave me a more rounded concept of what the expectations would be when I grew up. I was lucky to have these role models of working women to compare and contrast with my mother, who chose to stay at home while I was young. My mother and I have had conversations about this, and I totally get her rationale. If she had to work to support us, she would have, but the financial pressure wasn't there, so she didn't feel the need.

My mother was accepted and attended NJIT right after high school. My Grandma Dorothy, wanted both her girls to be professional women. So she took it upon herself to find a profession that would work for her daughter, who enjoyed and was talented in sketching and drawing. My grandmother enrolled my mother in the drafting program there. My mother was handed a bag with all the supplies she would need as she was being informed of the program she was about to embark on. My mother attended and did well academically but expressed that the social pressure was just too much for her at the time. She was the only female in all of her classes. Mom recalled as her heels clicked as she walked down the hall, the guys would come out of the classrooms to watch her pass and after the first semester was over, she dropped out. That would have made me nervous as well.

Mom has done a great job over the years helping my sisters and I feel as if we met and knew our grandparents and uncle, who were gone before any of us were born. Mom was the youngest in the family and most likely an "oops" because she was eight years younger than her sister and ten years younger than her brother. She always told us stories about what a dedicated and amazing mother she had. She told us how Grandma Dorothy – lacking bus fare and with a heart condition – walked a few miles in the snow

49

one day to bring my mother boots – fearing my mom's feet would get cold and wet coming home from work during the snowstorm. My grandmother passed away a month after that walk. Mom's dad, a quiet and stern father, was born in 1900, fought in World War 1, and was awarded a Purple Heart for an injury sustained in action. Grandpa Michael was older than my Grandma Dorothy by a bit. He would bring my mother home a piece of candy after work. As a little girl, she would use her dancing skills to entertain his friends for tips at the local tavern. In the summers, he and my mom traveled by train to visit his sisters in Pennsylvania. My mother spent time with her cousin, Dolores, during those trips and they stayed close through the years. My family would visit Dolores's family when we were young children. Through the year, I became close with Dolores's son, my cousin Mark. Mark was two weeks away from being ordained a priest when he decided that wasn't the life he wanted. Mark helped me through a difficult time later in my life when I was struggling after ending a relationship with my spiritual advisor. Mark helped me come through that without losing my faith in the church altogether.

Before the "Jaws of Life" were invented, my Grandpa Michael once literally ripped the door off a car when someone was trapped inside. Shortly before he passed away in the winter of 1959, he fell off a tugboat at work into the Hudson River and never told a soul. The family found out at the wake when his co-workers told them the story. Both grandparents got cold and wet in the winter right before passing. A similar ending came to my dad. He had been duck hunting in the winter, shortly before he passed as well.

Mom's brother, Teddy, passed away from Leukemia as a very young man. Mom's vignettes always reflected that Uncle Teddy was always kind to her and would take her along to the movies with his friends when she was small. She once played a trick on him and cooked him a hamburger made of dog food and he ate it. Her brother was only truly angry with her that one time. My mother and uncle shared a love of baseball and my mom often reminisces on the last conversation she had with him. He was in the hospital the day he passed, October 1, 1961 – the day Roger Maris broke Babe Ruth's record for home runs, hitting his sixty-first in a season. This was something that my mother and uncle would banter back and forth about throughout the baseball season, the push and pull between Roger Maris and Mickey Mantle to break the record. My uncle rooted for Maris to break the record, and my mom was a huge Mantle fan, always furious because the pitchers would walk Mantle to shut him down. This back and forth tug-of-war gave them something to bond over. On the day he passed, my mom said she was happy that my uncle had that victory. He was weak in the hospital bed, but their last conversation – discussing how Maris broke Ruth's record – put the last smile on my uncle's face. An uncle I never met, but I know because my mother always kept her family alive through her stories.

The difference between my mother and me was that I didn't believe I had the option to rely on anyone to take care of me, and when I had Alex and found myself on my own, it was always full steam ahead for me. I really didn't leave myself many options. Once I got started, I've never really stopped, always trying to level up with the idea of making it an easier lift for my own children. I don't know if it's worked out that way for them, but that has always been my motivation for my kids and their future.

Both options have value, and seeing both sides was definitely to my advantage as a future woman who would do the juggling act of working with babies and small kids at home. I'm happy that my daughter-in-law, Amanda, is able to stay home and raise my two grandchildren, Eleni and Leo. They are thriving and it is a blessing that they don't need to be dropped at daycare every morning.

Dana and I have noticed through the years that our lives have had a similar ebb and flow in play. We both had baby siblings around the same ages. We both had to be inventive, problem-solvers along the way. Neither of us are prescribed to doing everything exactly as expected. We've faced oddly related issues at times in our lives, but no matter what, Dana has been there for me when I've needed a friend, especially when few were to be found in my early twenties.

As little girls, we would take our bikes down to her dad's house and visit with her stepmother, Terri, and her little brothers. Terri was very funny and would talk with us about boys. We had a running joke. Terri would ask what we've been up to, and I'd say, "Fox Hunting." Later realizing this may have been GOD's funny way of foreshadowing where I would meet Alex years later. It was silly but, at the time, very funny. I remember having a big laugh with Terri every time we orchestrated this little banter. Dana's dad was a police officer, and whenever there was any trouble noted over the police radio about activities around the Woodrow schoolyard, he'd show up, find Dana and whoever else she was with, and deliver us home.

Dana and I decided to try to make some money and shared a route delivering the Bayonne Community News throughout the Boulevard Gardens Apartments. There was a lot of work involved in the prep and the delivery. We had to roll the papers and put each one in a rubber band, and if bad weather was looming, put the papers in a plastic bag as well. Our job was to put a newspaper in front of each door in this garden apartment complex. Each building was three stories, and we had to run up and down the stairs in each building. While we would split up the route, it still took us many hours. There were weeks when we'd listen to the devil instead of the angel over our shoulders, and we'd dump some of the papers down the sewer and skip some of the side streets on our route. We would take some of the money we earned and buy Arctic Light cigarettes and practice smoking, the seed from which my teenage nickname, "Cigarette," was born.

I was no stranger to smoking. My Grandma Jessie would have me buy Kent 100s for her. She'd also have me light the matches for her so she could get that initial drag going. My grandmother had very advanced rheumatoid arthritis and could barely use her hands, so I would help her get her cigarettes lit.

We had a hiding place for our Arctic Lights. It was in a drain pipe sticking off a utility pole in our neighborhood on Avenue B. We had a lot of fun together and learned a lot about growing up. We had a couple of big fights too. One was over which direction we had to go to get home when I was out on an errand for my mom, picking up a package from the Sears Catalog pickup center on Broadway. I always had a hard time with directions, and Dana had to literally walk me uptown two blocks to show me that the street numbers were getting higher and prove that was the way we needed to go to get back home. Another time we had a big debate about girls and their menstrual cycle. I was absolutely convinced that everyone in the world had their period on the same exact days.

We were arguing in her room for quite a while about it. Dana was trying to convince me, but I wouldn't budge. Then her older sister, Lisa, who was listening to this ridiculous fight, came into the bedroom and set me straight. Thank you, Lisa! I have many happy memories from those still innocent times. Sometimes, Dana's mom, Carol, would let me come along when they were going shopping. One particular day we went to Daffy Dan's on Route 1&9 and had been out shopping all day. Dana was trying on clothes for back to school all day and was given the job of carrying the bags with all the day's finds. She was instructed not to take her eyes off of the bags, and somehow we left the bags somewhere, and when we went back for them, they were gone. Dana's mom was furious. I'll never forget the ride back home that day. I think it was the day she swayed the car and almost ran over a neighbor who used to annoy her.

One night we had an impromptu party at Dana's house. It was similar to a "Project X" situation. The party got out of control fast. An Oriental rug was damaged. Someone spilled a drink, and the edge curled up; high-end wine was missing, and a match collection that Mrs. B had been procuring for years was desecrated. To say the least, we were in a lot of trouble. Carol called my mother to come over and survey the damage. We were both punished for a while, but it was the first of many memorable parties put on by Dana through our almost fifty years of friendship.

I had a lot of really great times with Dana and her mom. Carol worked at the Meadowlands Racetrack and worked for the executive who ran the whole operation. Dana would often bring me along to go to concerts. I remember seeing Elton John, Madonna, Rod Stewart, The Rolling Stones, Bruce Springsteen, Bon Jovi, and so many more. Dana's mom would also offer me Devils hockey tickets when Alex was small so I could bring him to see hockey games. I would really get into going to those games as well. There were times when we'd go to work with Mrs. B on weekends, and we'd hang out and watch the horse races. Sometimes Dana and I would even be able to slide a bet in here and there with a worker that knew her mom. It was a different time that would never be able to happen today.♥

The years went by, and as it happened, I moved from being closest with Jill and Dana to Candace and Michelle. Through the years, we were all friends and part of the same bigger group of high school kids that hung around the Woodrow schoolyard. My friendship with Candace and Michelle took me away from Dana and Jill for some time, but we were all friends together for many years.

Things happened between Candace, Michelle, and me that ended our friendship for good. The parts of this book when I mention somehow always feeling less, and not quite as smart or as good, comes back here for me. I realized these were friendships that I needed to let go of to move on with my life and become who I was destined to be. These people were reinforcing a narrative for me that I did not see. However, I would be remiss not to give Candace's mom a heartfelt nod. She treated me with kindness and was firm when she felt she needed to be, as a true teacher would be, which she was. She didn't get mad when I ate all the Wheat Thins. Instead, she started buying extra for me, as well as onion dip. Once or twice she even made chicken cacciatore when I asked her to. She made chocolate chip cookies and watched movies with us. She was willing to bring as many kids as she could pack into her long white 80's Ford Thunderbird to Sandy Hook beach for the day. I slept over so many nights that Janet purchased a loveseat sleeper bed for Candace's room.

After being invited on a trip to the Bahamas with Candace's family, I saved up the money to go by working at my job scrubbing shirt collars, washing, and then ironing one hundred shirts or more each week at The Tux Shop. After my job scrubbing floors in the apartment building, I was now leveling up to being a laundry lady. Again, the chip on my shoulder was getting bigger. I saw my friends being kids and their parents providing for them without them having to really work hard for anything. I had already been struggling for money for over five years, and at this point, I was fourteen. Between the job cleaning the three-story apartment building hallways on Saturdays at age ten, to delivering newspapers, and the job at the Tux Shop – this is where self-reliance took hold. It gave me a chip on my shoulder as a younger person, but really it gave me the ability to be able to pick myself up and carry on – no matter what – throughout my life, because I have always depended on myself and tried to ask as little as possible of anyone.

Having too much pride and an inability to ask for help has been a wall in my way. But I have overcome that as well. Becoming humble and admitting I need help at times has been something I've had to work on in my life, but once I was able to humble myself and show people my vulnerability, things changed for me. As a result, my life and career grew exponentially. Being able to show people, especially my students, my vulnerability has been a great teaching tool. When I tell my students, "I don't know, but let's look it up and find the answer together," that's a real teachable moment. When the students know you are learning with them or taking the role of lead learner or facilitator, the students will become totally engaged and focused, and try to grasp the knowledge along with their teacher. Kids don't like being talked down to, but when you empower them to learn side by side with you, that's really powerful.

I had been putting my money for the Bahamas trip in an envelope in a kitchen drawer at Candace's house and told Candace and her mom what I was doing to save up. Somehow there was a miscommunication, and the money I had been saving was not in the drawer one day when I went to add to it. It was an amount of money that I couldn't replace in time for the trip. I know it wasn't on purpose, but when the money wasn't there, no one remembered when I told them I had been putting money in an envelope in a drawer in the kitchen. I still owed three hundred dollars at the time, and I had to ask my parents for the money because my envelope savings were gone. I only made about one hundred dollars a week at the time and wouldn't have time to acquire the balance on my own. My dad gave me the money, but I didn't have much extra spending money needed for the trip. I overheard Candace's dad complain about my parents, asking rhetorically how they could send me to the Bahamas with so little money for food, etc. That made me feel really unwelcome and hurt, especially because of the misunderstanding of the missing money in the draw, which would have made a difference.

Another comment that always stood out to me was when I was asked to go on the trip. It was presented to me as "a chance of a lifetime" and I "may never have this opportunity again." Why on Earth would someone think that I wouldn't be able to make it to the Bahamas during my lifetime? This just drove home the perception of the options that were available to me. This sentiment seemed to pervade how people perceived what I could accomplish or what was expected of me.

Because of all these things, I was feeling bitter and salty at the same time. So when a guy working in the resort's casino asked me to go on a date, I accepted. Janet and Candace were not happy with that decision. Rightly so. I was way too young to be leaving the area with a strange guy. Yet I went because of the way I was feeling. I later realized I was looking to show them I didn't need them as much as they thought – wanting to prove I could have my own experiences on this "trip of a lifetime."

That guy took me to his apartment and tried to take advantage of me. Luckily, as always, I fought him off and was able to get out of there. I found my way back to the resort area where we were staying and told Janet and Candace what happened to me. They were truly relieved that I was alright, but I think that was when

Candace and I started to unravel. It took years, but the bonds that held us were loosening. I was just not on the same trajectory as her. The road I had to take, and my options, were different from Candace's. I knew I wanted to get somewhere, but I also knew my path would be different.

When you are a kid with fewer options and opportunities, it's a double edge sword when you have friends who have more than you do... by a lot. Exposure to a better lifestyle is a good opportunity for future self-efficacy goals. But it can also exasperate negative self-esteem in the moment. The feelings of having less or being less important or worthy, creep in. Many kids came through our house whose parents were not in the same financial position as we were once we both completed school and began our careers. A friend of Alex's actually robbed our restaurant cash register one night by throwing a brick through the front window. A police detective uncovered this. We didn't press charges. However, this boy's church-going mother was so angry with us. She told me over the course of this whole event that it was our fault this happened to her son because we gave our son everything and that her son was so jealous he didn't know how to deal with his emotions. Supposedly, our overindulgence was the cause of her son's mistake. This was a single mother who was obviously struggling, but I knew she had a point. Her son would see all the things that Alex had because he had two families to indulge him. On top of that, I was often guilty of overcompensating because of my own experiences and not wanting my kids to grow up feeling like they were less worthy or less important than I had felt.

Wanting to expand my children's horizons was something that was always on my mind. Fusing this with the fact that I always had the travel bug from the time I told Jill and her family that I drove to Hawaii with my family, it is no wonder that I made sure my family boarded transcontinental flights. But the comment about the Bahamas trip being an opportunity of a lifetime was probably the impetus for the many vacations Anthony and I have taken with our family. A goal of mine was to make sure that my children were given a taste of traveling within and outside the US while young, so that they would have an adventurous nature when they grew up and were raising their own children. From the time they were babies, I had a large world map on the wall over the top bunk bed in their room. We'd read books at night, find the destinations mentioned in the books, and just talk about different places in the world.   All three of my children have traveled inside and outside the US with the family and later without the family – whether through work, school, or with friends. The feelings of resentment I felt in my youth were again flipped into a goal accomplished. The seeds were planted with those comments that sowed many memories to treasure and future adventures for generations to come.

Gia toured Ireland and England in high school, Jake has traveled to Paris, Canada, and California with friends, and Alex has been to Japan, Norway, and many other regions in the Arctic through work. He currently lives in Alaska with his family, and we have all been there to visit him several times.

My daughter-in-law Amanda's family are exceptionally interesting people who run "Devil's Mountain Lodge" in Nabesna, Alaska, which is seven hours north of Anchorage. Here you can be guided on hunting expeditions, take a flight in one of their planes to witness from above the vastness of Alaska, the mountain formations, glaciers, and wildlife while being given a detailed explanation of the history observed through the geological formations of the scenery you observe as Kirk, my grandchildren's grandfather, flies you through the wilds of Alaska. He has the ability to land his plane on a variety of mountain tops or valleys in between the mountains. He will accompany you if you would like to get out and walk on the permafrost and search for fossils. When we were there, he took us to "Flattop Mountain," which is a mesa, an elevated area of land with steep sides. My son, Alex, was annoyed with me because I didn't want to walk to the very edge with him. He forgot about the time a few years prior when he took me to the highest mountain top in the Anchorage area, and the wind nearly blew me off the side of the mountain. There was no guardrail, and Alex literally grabbed my coat and pulled me back from being blown off by the high winds.

On this mesa, we were treated to a barbeque of moose burgers with all the fixings prepared by Gennie, Amanda's mom who is an amazing and interesting person,, and my co-grandma. They will leave you there for a day or a week if you want to hunt or hike or just meditate in the wilderness.

Kirk, his brother, Cole, or someone else they have working with them, will come back for you when you are ready. They will leave you alone or with a guide; that is up to you. If you are alone, you will have a two-way radio so that if there is a problem, Kirk will come and save the day, just as he did when we were traveling up to the lodge in the summer of 2022.

We were in heavy-duty, four-wheel drive trucks traveling over river beds that were overflowing from the rains and the snow melting and running down the mountains. We had crossed over a few riverbeds already, and it was very tense. Anthony was driving a big pickup truck that Kirk lent us and had to slam it into high four-wheel drive and angle the truck to come at the riverbank to the right because there was more ground for the tires to grab in that particular direction to get over it. We couldn't take the chance with Alex's pickup, which was not as high or as super duty as Kirk's. We had to stop in the middle of the woods and wait it out overnight. This was one of the most frightening nights of my life. Each time we had to relieve ourselves, we had to get out of the truck and risk encountering a bear or other wildlife. We had no way of contacting Amanda's parents at the lodge because there was no Wi-Fi or internet service in the woods.

Amanda had forgotten to make contact at the last point before Wi-Fi wouldn't be available any longer, so her family wasn't sure of our arrival time. Alex didn't seem too concerned but wanted to wait till morning to see if the amount of water running through the river beds would slow down so that we could cross safely. Alex and Amanda's two small babies were passengers in this truck, and we didn't want to risk a catastrophe. After spending a frightening night, soon after dawn a plane flew over us, and we knew Amanda's dad was out looking for and had located us. About an hour after that, he came driving up over the river banks with an even bigger heavy-duty truck than the one he lent us, and we transferred all the luggage and provisions from Alex's truck to this super-super heavy duty truck which could make it over the river bank. We left Alex's pickup there about an hour away from the lodge on a dirt road that cuts through the woods. Kirk had discussed with Anthony exactly how to come at it; there was a driving skill needed to get this done. I can drive a car, but there is no way I could have driven that truck over that riverbed in the way that it needed to be done to get us over. It was really, really scary. We made it over, but not without the exhaust system on the truck that Anthony was driving, being ripped off... and later retrieved by Kirk.

This was an amazing adventure that we were able to have twice. There are small cabins built and placed throughout their vast homestead for people to use for shelter and to cook while spending time out in the vastness alone or with their group. As a democrat, and full-bred city girl – after experiencing this – my understanding of why the Constitution's Second Amendment is so important to people who live and work in truly untouched and rural parts of our country and is a major issue for safety and sustenance as well.

Collectively we have covered a lot of ground over the years. Together we visited Italy, Greece, Turkey, Bermuda, Puerto Rico, the Bahamas, Jamaica, Dominican Republic, and many other spots in the Caribbean. Anthony and I have been to Cancun and Vegas alone, but besides those two trips, we have traveled with our family. We spent a week in Katy, Texas, outside of Houston, with my dad's brother, Uncle Gerald, his wife, Aunt Kay, and our cousin Kyle over the summer of 2007. My son, Jake, still remembers the BBQ ribs my uncle meticulously made on his grill for us. Jake stands firm that they were the best ribs he's ever eaten in his life. They made this a really special trip and took our family on a two-night journey through southeast Texas, visiting NASA, the Alamo, SeaWorld, San Antonio's Riverwalk, and down toward the Gulf of Mexico to a coastal town, Kemah, which was destroyed the next year in 2008 by Hurricane Ike.

My Uncle Gerald was the first person in the family to leave Hudson County, New Jersey. He was the inspiration for Alex to leave the area to go to college at Western Kentucky University and become a Hilltopper, earning both his undergraduate and master's degrees there, just as my uncle did in the 1960s. This was the beginning of my son's journey to his wife, Amanda, who he met in Alaska, where he relocated to live for work.

Gia and I spent two weeks in France in 2019 during the World Cup festivities. We didn't attend the games, but the activity around Paris was something I'll never forget. Witnessing how the city of Paris went wild when France won the World Cup was staggering. We went to many museums and churches, wine tastings, and a private dinner cooked by a French chef just for us on a rooftop overlooking the church at the highest point in Paris, Sacré Coeur Basilica of the Sacred Heart of Paris. We took tours of Van Gogh's neighborhood and the places he spent time, and we toured churches and learnt about how to read a building's facade to know who lived there one to two hundred years ago. These were trips of a lifetime that I had been dreaming about since I was a young girl.

We saw so many things and just spent time together walking around Paris, going to the Eiffel Tower almost every day, and preparing picnics on its grounds. We were surprised when going to the grocery store to buy snacks. The differences between the food selections between the US and France were vast. I will always remember the aisle with hundreds of different cheeses. France's equivalent to our Kraft Cheese is President Cheese, which, where I usually shop, is the better cheese. I found that amusing. Salmon is another staple and occupies an entire aisle in the same very long deli case dedicated to different types of salmon. We were shocked to find out that in France, they do not sell any type of non-stick spray for frying or sautéing, because hydrogenated oils are banned in France.

We were looking for that to make breakfast at the Airbnb. While we didn't see many overweight people, many people walked around nibbling on twelve to sixteen-inch baguettes in the mornings with their coffee. When we went to cafes, and people heard our accent, we were asked, "What is happening in America?" They then would snicker and say negative things about Trump. It was during the news cycle when he had been caught on tape talking about grabbing women's pussies. It was embarrassing and definitely not a good look for the US at that time. I just shrugged my shoulders and said, "I didn't vote for him."

As we were leaving for the airport, I was running around checking everything – passports, luggage, etc. – and I left my cell phone at home by accident. I didn't realize it until we were going through TSA at the airport, and it was too late to go back or have someone bring it to me. We were essentially unplugged and only had one phone to share. Then, a Starbucks Frappuccino with a loose cap in her computer bag rendered Gia's new Macbook out of commission. It turned out to be a blessing because we just focused on where we were and the opportunity to take it all in as much as possible, and we didn't worry about staying in touch with home or being on the computer in the evening.

Chapter 7: Listening To What is Really Being Said

One thing that really impacted me was when my life got very messy for a period of time and I went to talk with Janet about it. The concern she showed wasn't for me, but for how my life had impacted Candace's in the recent past. It was as if she had an epiphany during that conversation, and anything that wasn't working out for her daughter had to do with my messy life's fallout raining down on her and the level of anxiety that my life must have caused her. This couldn't have been the furthest thing from the truth. At that time, Candace had completely deleted me from her life. I had absolutely nothing to do with anything she was doing. When I was invited to her bridal shower and wedding, I was seated in the "had been" friend section – I was a "C-lister," not even a "B-lister." It was an after-after thought to even have me there, as the swinging door hit my chair as the trays went in and out of the kitchen. The message of where I landed in her line-up was loud and clear, and I'm certain that Candace didn't lose one second of sleep worrying about me when I was going through the messy years of my life.

When I walked away from that last talk I had with Janet, I was devastated and felt worse than when I had arrived. After I told her all about my problem with Alex being legally awarded into his dad's custody, she offered to lend me money if I left my jewelry with her as collateral. Of course, I thanked her but refused. That just killed me. After that day, things just were never the same for me in my heart. When I was invited to Candace's wedding, it was a time when Anthony and I were extremely broke, and the word was out about how expensive "each head" was. Customary Jersey etiquette is to cover your head or heads at weddings with a cash gift. Bringing a material gift isn't something typically done. We simply weren't in a financial position to cover the plates. I didn't even have enough money to buy a new outfit. I wore an ivory-colored pantsuit with gold accents that I bought a decade earlier in the early nineties and had the shoulder pads removed. I thought it was a nice outfit for this upscale wedding. As we walked past the receiving line, Janet said to me, "You and Candace are in the same color," as if that was a problem. Maybe it was? I'm not sure. All I know is it was a pantsuit and definitely didn't feel like I was upstaging the bride.

When I think of Candace, I wish her no ill will. We had many good times together but I can't take the rap for what happened there. My life's trajectory wasn't something she wanted on her radar and I felt a vibe from her that I had disappointed her the times we were together once my life got messy. Candace was going north and I was going south.

What I will take is the lesson that everyone has their own lens they look through life with, and I can't fault Janet for having the lens as mother to Candace, because that was who she was, first and foremost. Mama Claws can be very sharp indeed. But, if she truly considered me someone important in her heart, her reactions and what she said to me would have been quite different. Again, there is a takeaway here. We've had more than a few young adults come through our home through the years with different situations, and based on the interaction of that day with Janet, I purposefully responded to these young people by pulling directly from what happened during that one encounter. Again, always purposefully looking to repurpose past negatives in my mind to become lessons learned and turn positives into negatives.

Ultimately, the pain and humiliation I experienced growing up was my payment for the good it would produce for others down the line in my purposeful repurposing plan. Whenever the moment strikes, I am ready to pull from my war chest and use it to lift someone up and out of whatever it may be that I'm called to act upon.

Very few people in my life have actually shocked me. My former friend, Michelle, was one of those people. During the years when Candace was out of touch Michelle and I stood very close. So much so that Michelle is Jake's Godmother. However, the lesson she taught me is that a true friend wouldn't have done what she did to me. It was my short memory and inability to hold a grudge that led me to forgive once but the second time I just couldn't remain friends with her. Later on I'll explain more about what happened the first time. The second time was just too much and isn't worth the time to tell. The lesson is, look out for fake friends. Having no friends is an upgrade.

Chapter 8: Lessons My Kids Taught Me

My own children have taught me so many lessons. To have faith, to be tough and gritty, to stop, to be sensitive and vulnerable, to be willing to feel emotions that are difficult, and to shut off when it is absolutely necessary. My kids have taught me all these things. My three children are my entire world, and without each one of them, I wouldn't be the person I am today. Every single thing I did for myself, I did for them – to make sure that they had every opportunity that was within reason for them growing up in our working- to lower-middle-class family. My hobby was providing my children with engaging outings that would open up their minds, such as trips to college plays and museums when they were younger. Giving them experiences, keeping them busy on weekends, spending time with my sister, Dena, and sister-in-law, Lisa, and raising our children all together. We had a lot of fun doing nothing but being together.

When we first started out, Anthony worked for his parents on the Mister Softee truck, which was his parents' family business. Anthony had a route in Jersey City from Claremont to Communipaw Avenues, which stretched from Rt. 440 to Bergen Avenue. For most of the year, he would be driving up and down the streets of Jersey City selling soft serve treats to the kids in the Greenville section. Usually, with Dena or Lisa, we would drive around looking for Anthony to get the kids ice cream. We would spend the day at the park and then have the kids in "lockdown" in their car seats, go through Wendy's drive-thru for dinner, and then go looking for Anthony so that the kids could have a slush or cone before the night was over.

There were many days when Dena and I would spend the entire day outside, from the park to bowling at the Knights of Columbus, to dinner at Wendy's or pizza, and then to look for Anthony on the truck. Dena and I were like Lucy and Ethel as a team. We were always planning and doing something. The kids all grew up together. It was great; Alex and our nephew, Tommy, Gia, and Demi, and Jake and Justin were the crew. We were always together. Dena and Lisa often worked on Saturdays, being employed in service industries, so I had the entire crew for many weekends.

Lisa and I bought season passes to Great Adventure one year, and we went every week that summer. Jake, Demi, and Gia were babies in the carriage, but Alex and Tommy had a blast. We always had impromptu family get-togethers and barbequed hamburgers and hot dogs with mac and cheese a few times a month, if not weekly. We often reminisce about the five-pound bag of chicken nuggets we'd buy from BJ's weekly and the large canister of cheese balls. My kids went to the doctor for a blood test and had high cholesterol. The sad faces because of the healthy foods that followed that diagnosis remain funny to this day. Grilled chicken and London broil were not favorites of my children. Every time I brought out the pot to make chicken soup, they would cry and beg me not to because they knew they'd have to eat it for days. We didn't have enough money at the time and would lean heavily on our credit cards to make sure the kids had what they needed and wanted.

I was just starting out as a teacher making $32,000 in 2001. We thought that was fantastic! We finally had a stable income and health benefits. One of the first things we did was purchase an above-ground pool for the kids. It was surrounded by mud and grass, and the kids would slip and slide in the mud and then jump in the pool to clean off because the tray to rinse their feet before getting in wasn't enough. Our family dog, Honey, a cocker spaniel, was part of our family as well. She even had a dog cousin, Candy, who would come over at times with Lisa and Demi. We picked Honey out as a little puppy. This runt of her litter became part of our family and grew up with the kids. She ate through walls and even ate an essay Anthony had been working on for his X-ray program for hours. It was handwritten in a notebook at the time. She loved to jump in and out of the pool with the kids all day.

She would bark incessantly when the pool was open, and the neighbors would complain. One day she swallowed so much water she almost drowned and had to be rushed to the vet. She was back in that pool a few days later. She never stopped wanting to go in the pool, even until her last summer with us in 2017.

In the summer of 2003, we went on our first and only trip to Disney World in Orlando, Florida. Anthony had just sold the

Mister Softee Truck and was going back to school at Essex County Community College to become an X-Ray technician. Now that I was settled into my position as a teacher, he was going to take three years to go to school, be there to pick up the kids from school, do homework, and make dinner. It was a good arrangement. I worked the Casper after-school program every day and was making extra money to bolster my entry-level teacher salary. After the lean years leading up to this, we felt we were doing alright and had finally begun to get where we wanted to be. I had never been to Disney World. We stayed in a family motel in Kissimmee outside of Disney because we surely were not at the point where we could afford to stay on Disney property. We were thrilled to be able to make this trip with our kids. We set off at night; Anthony felt driving overnight would be easier because the kids would sleep for most of the trip. They did, but there were hiccups over the road and not too many hours into the trip, Alex was sitting up front in our car, and I was sitting in the backseat with my feet on the hump in the back, with my knees up in my chest, separating Jake and Gia from fighting with each other. Obviously, when we arrived, Anthony needed to sleep, so we spent time in the game room and the pool at the motel during the first day there. Once Anthony slept and recharged, we were off to Disney World on our second day in Florida. We went to the park and bought a three-day Hopper Pass. As we were walking up to the Magic Kingdom, I took it in for the first time as we came around the walking path, and I saw Cindarella's Castle in the distance overlooking the entire park. I looked around at all the flowers hanging on the high fences and the bushes and flowers carefully manicured into different shapes, the people in costume, and the thousands of people buzzing around – everyone happy and smiling, families enjoying themselves. I felt that I had made it at that moment, that all my hard work was paying off. I remember tearing up and feeling very emotional, but I was wiping away my tears because I didn't want Anthony or the kids to see me crying. I didn't want them to see what a really big deal this was for me. I just wanted them to feel like everyone else.

We entered the park and started to take it all in. We went on all the must-do rides such as It's a SmallWorld, Tower of Terror, the Aerosmith Rock 'n' Roller Coaster, the log flume, and so many others. As always, we were watching our budget, buying our kids the souvenirs they wanted, within reason. We felt we could only afford one fan that sprays mist to keep cool, so we shared it; we also shared one turkey leg. I'll never forget standing in a circle, each of us taking a bite off that turkey leg and then Gia finishing it off. Gia has always loved dark meat. We never have to fight about who will get the breast meat in our house. There is always enough because Gia loves the legs and thighs. That first day at Disney was great. We have a picture of Alex carrying Gia out of the park that day. She was so exhausted that she passed out in his arms. Alex is ten years older than Gia. When Gia was young, they were close; Alex would walk Jake and Gia to school, and his girlfriend, Laura, would pick them up.

They aren't as close today because Gia is liberal and progressive and living as a transgender male. Alex is a patriotic conservative man who is living his life his way, making no apologies. Jake as the middle child, is the middleman and sounding board for everyone. My kids love each other but can be at odds.

After the first day, we ate dinner somewhere outside the park and went back to the motel where the kids were having great success with a claw machine in the game room. They were winning everything in the machine. Alex cleaned that machine out of laser pointers and pogs and whatever else were fad items of the day. We assumed the setting on the machine must have been off because when we went back to the game room the next day, they had fixed it, and it wasn't giving out prizes nearly at the same rate.

The second day, at Blizzard Beach, was one of the most stressful, traumatic, and draining days of my life. Alex was fourteen at the time and extremely into playing Warhammer. He was adamant about going to a Warhammer studio that he had looked up. It was about an hour from Orlando, so we brought him that morning and doubled back to Blizzard Beach. We went on different water rides and waded into little pools and lazy rivers. As we came across the Lily Pad area, of course, the kids wanted to go jump from one supersized floating green leaf to the next all the way across the pool, and then run around and do it again. We were standing there watching them both. Jake was going across saying, "Mommy, look, look, watch me!" and Gia did the same, "Look, Daddy, this is so much fun!" We were both watching them go around and around as they crossed over the obstacle course and then ran back around to do it again. Then Jake called me over to watch him jump from one lily pad to the next, close-up, so I walked maybe fifteen feet to watch him. I took my eyes off Gia coming around for maybe fifteen seconds. When I looked up, I didn't see her running around the back of the pool or around to enter from the front again. I started running back and forth, looking for her, but I couldn't find her. Now I was yelling to Anthony to look for her, and was getting very upset because I couldn't see her, and it's been over two minutes now. The trip from getting out of the water back around might be thirty seconds, so I knew something was wrong. I jumped into the pool and started flipping the lily pads up to look under each one, thinking she may be caught under one and drowning. She wasn't in the pool and was nowhere to be found. By now I was hysterical, and Anthony was on high alert and very scared. Jake was just standing there because I told him to get out and stay in one place as we looked for Gia.

At this point, maybe four minutes into this scene, Anthony said, "I'm going to security to see if someone has found her. You stay right here and wait for her to come back here." We are now feeling as if she may have been kidnapped since she literally disappeared into thin air. The fear and terror in my heart during those moments were literally stopping me from being able to breathe.

I was completely frozen and scared to my core, my insides felt as if they were draining, and I was holding myself up just to keep looking for her everywhere. I was standing on the steps to have a better vantage point to look into the pool for Gia, possibly floating or caught under one of the lily pads. I was hunched over because I simply couldn't hold myself upright. I was completely collapsing from the fear and terror of the situation as I was standing there, not saying anything to Jake, realizing later that he must have been very traumatized as well. In his own way, at six years old, he was trying to help bring me back to some level of clear thinking. At that moment, I kept looking under the lily pads hoping I'd find her there, but also scared because it would have been too long to be underwater without air. Hunched over the railing, crying at a level that I have never cried before or after, Jake came over and said, "Mommy, you're just going to have to forget about her." That was it; I completely lost my mind and started yelling at him, "How could you say that? Don't ever say that! How could I ever forget about your sister?"

Those forty-five minutes most likely took several years off my life. The level of terror and fear felt by a parent when they have lost a small child can't be explained. Gia was three and a half when that happened, and every time I think about it, my heart starts to race, my chest gets hot and aches, and I feel uneasy waves of fear pulsing through my body.

Shortly after Jake told me I'd have to forget about her, Anthony came walking back with our little Gia in his arms. My heart just eases up thinking about when I laid my eyes on him walking toward us with her. All she had to say was, "I wasn't lost; I made a friend." She had somehow drifted over to the left and went up to the super high slippery slide, but when she got to the top, she was stopped by a Disney cast member. Why it had to come to all that, I'll never know. Gia insists to this day that she told Jake where she was going and that she was pointing out her parents to the worker on the top of the slide, but we were told there is a protocol that must be followed when a small child is found unattended.

When Anthony went to security, this was long before cell phones, he told me he was reunited with her within a few minutes, but the process to release her to him took quite a while. Jake and I were standing around that pool thinking the worst. It was a day I'll never forget as long as I live. Yet it taught me something, just like the day when I felt as if a lightning bolt hit my head when my mom was having an epic meltdown – the same night the angel came to our closet. Jake also was reacting to me and my hysteria, trying to bring it down a notch by shutting off all feelings and going into survival mode. Jake was in survival mode. Everything is urgent right now; I must forget Gia, now, this minute, so that we can move on. Classic survival mode.

My poor Jake, it was a similar scene to what happened all those years ago with my mom. I did the same thing to Jake that day by not being able to control my emotions, and he saw me lose total control. He was six; I was about six as well. When a child sees a parent go to that level, it can be very traumatizing for that child. However, I learned to understand my mom, myself, and others better that day after reflecting on that situation and the emotions and reactions that came from it. All parents can be unhinged at times but it took that day at Blizzard Beach to teach me that.

Not that day, but as time marched on, that moment seared into my life's memory. It's a tentpole I carry with me as a barometer for my emotions. That was a low point for me. It grounded me in always thinking from the perspective of, you just don't know what people are dealing with in their lives. Parents come into schools acting irate, but you don't know what they are dealing with at home. As human beings, we must give each other some room and try to step back and let someone yell and get it off their chest. If you can be that person to stand back and receive it, that may just be what the other person really needs at that moment. It's hard to humble yourself, but the rewards can be astounding, the friends you can make in a moment like that if you let that person get it out.

Other lessons Gia has helped me learn, like Alex, revolve around reading. With all three of my children, reading was always something I did with all of them at night as I put them to bed. By now, with Jake and Gia, I was a much better reader than I had started out with Alex and the Golden Books from ShopRite. Jake and Gia were members of the Book of the Month Club and had all the children's books the house could hold. In these years, I was buying books for my children and for my students as well. One night as I was reading *"Where the Wild Things Are"* by Maurice Sendak to Gia after many past readings of this book. At three years old, Gia corrected me. "Mommy, you say gnashing" – leaving off the "g" sound. I had been pronouncing the "g" in this consonant digraph or phoneme, not knowing that when g and n are together, the g is silent. That was a moment where I just stopped and couldn't believe my three-year-old had a better grip on decoding rules than I did. She told me that her teacher didn't pronounce the g.

I was embarrassed, but I also knew my situation and how difficult reading had been for me when I was young. I wasn't a big reader of fiction, which uses a different palate of descriptive words. Reading textbooks with teacher jargon was easier than a novel for me up to this point. There were and still are holes in my vocabulary. Obviously, if you are not reading descriptive passages, your descriptive vocabulary isn't expanding. There was a lot of work ahead for me, but I eventually did develop a desire to read much more and to purposefully grow over time. As a child, I definitely wasn't hearing the teachers' instructions, and the lessons were not getting through.

Gia was attending the childcare program at New Jersey City University (NJCU), which was a laboratory childcare center for the students of the university. Jake and Gia were very lucky to attend this amazing center. All the staff had PhDs or were working on earning advanced degrees. The children and their interactions through daily activities were the subjects of their research. It remains an amazing program to this day. Gia is a graduate student at NJCU and currently works as a graduate assistant for the university's Pride Center. They tell me that many young parents continue to depend on the program and give it high grades for outstanding childcare. I can attest to the fact that without NJCU's daycare program, I would not have been able to attend and graduate college with three young children, two of whom were not old enough for public school. Their program made it possible for me to go to school and earn the teaching degree that made my life today possible.

What impresses me about Gia is that even from such a young age, she had the ability to recognize when something wasn't right and had the boldness to let you know when something was wrong, just as she did with Mike. Gia has always had tenacity and isn't scared to open their mouth. I'm very proud of the person they have grown to be.

Knowing that I always had difficulty with spelling and sounding out unknown words, I started to look at my own reading difficulties differently. There was a lapse in my early reading instruction, coupled with dyslexia, that wasn't recognized. All this would fuel my desire to later earn a master's degree from Grand Canyon University in Curriculum and Instruction of Reading – finally slaying the beast with the knowledge of how it all happened. In turn, I have used the tools I learned and my personal knowledge of this particular struggle to help hundreds of students develop their reading skills through the years – simply doing for them the things that I know were overlooked in my case. Trying different strategies that are more kinesthetic, tactile, color orientated, and rhythmic while being patient, kind, talking softly, and moving slowly through lessons that are sensitive and difficult for students who favor alternative pathways to learning.

There was one time when I applied for a position at the school where I had worked for twenty years. At the point of this interview, I was there for about fifteen years and had my master's in reading for five years.

I felt I was the absolute shoo-in for this position. I had been teaching special education at this school for many years and had been successful teaching many disengaged readers to become fluent and confident in their reading. It seemed to be a natural progression for me to move to the next level in my career. There was a school posting for the position, and I submitted my resume and a cover letter discussing my abilities as a reading teacher and special education teacher. I felt there was an obvious connection between the two positions. Any student who would be in need of coaching in reading is in need of accommodations and modifications to the reading program that isn't working for them. Accordingly, I felt that my special education background only amplified my credentials as a reading specialist, showing that I've had many opportunities to hone my craft – making me even more qualified for the position. During the interview, the principal told me she didn't take my application seriously because, within my cover letter, I discussed my position as a special education teacher and not what I could do as a reading specialist. My stance was that the skills are intermingled, and the skills discussed in my cover letter were those that a Literacy Coach should possess. It was then that I recognized that I may never reach my goals and the narrative that I was working very hard to rewrite, if I just let it be. That was when I began marketing myself as a reading specialist available to work with individuals. I was able to help a series of clients ranging from children to adults. This gave me satisfaction because I was able to use my skills and knowledge in the way I wanted to. I was beginning to find ways to accomplish what I wanted to, with purpose, and not by chance. Believing in myself and what I knew I could do and not simply accepting the lane I was being put into at this point.

Chapter 9: Shaping Who I Would Be One Day

It was August of 1983, right before my senior year of high school began, when my son Alex's dad entered my life. We met in Foxes, a dance club in Jersey City. I was still dating Vinnie, who was a really nice, kind guy who came to visit me every day while I was home with Mono that year. Vinnie and I were going out for just over a year when I met Alex.

The day after I met Alex, I called Vinnie and broke up with him over the phone. It was a really messed up way to break up with someone that was so kind to me, and I know that I hurt him when I did that, but I believe it was all part of the master plan that GOD had for me. With Vinnie, I wasn't going to learn about life and develop a war chest of experiences in the same way. With him, I would have had a nice, calm life. The night I met Alex, my friend Candace and I hitched a ride home when we left Foxes. I was already doing dangerous things. I was sixteen, about to be seventeen in two months, and Alex was twenty-one. Yep,..first problem. When we began dating, I told him I was eighteen. "LOL." Eventually, he found out the truth. He would be coming over to my house for my birthday, and I was only turning seventeen. I had to come clean before he saw the cake on the table. He was shocked when I told him I was seventeen, another lie, and then a week later told him the truth that I was sixteen. He asked me, "Are you going to get any younger?" and I told him that was it. He charmingly told me, "I would never have dated someone this young, but I'm already in love with you." So, I felt a bit giddy and a little surprised, and we continued to date. He came to my house and, of course, my parents were very concerned because he was too old for me. But that wasn't his fault. I was in a club when I was sixteen with a fake ID I bought at Playland on 42nd Street in New York City. I looked the part, but really wasn't there yet. Alex told me he liked me because he knew I was "good" from the moment I took the joint from him in his car and held it as if it were a cigarette between my index and middle finger, instead of my thumb and index finger.

We were having a good time, and I was participating in things that I shouldn't have been. Alex was hiding a much more serious drug addiction from me that I was completely unaware of until much later in our relationship. There was a time when he would tell me he was going to Astoria, Queens, to buy his mother bread. I would take the ride with him, and he would tell me to stay in his van, keep the doors locked, and wait for him while he went to get the bread.

I honestly believed him. I'm literally laughing out loud at how naive I was. He told me if he didn't come back to call his friend, Ziggy, or his brother, Nick. Yet he always came back with a few loaves of bread to bring home to his mother.

During these years, I was exposed to a level of depravity that I don't think I would have ever come into contact with otherwise.

Again, I don't regret any of my experiences because all of them helped me understand and empathize with how people with addiction issues survive – and to the depth of personal destruction drug addiction can bring you. I saw things up close and personal and even experienced addiction myself.

Alex and I continued to date and he went to my senior prom with me. What I didn't know was that he had another girlfriend, the same age as me, with the same prom night as me. He decided to go with me and stood the other girl up. She ultimately got me back. Alex was DJ-ing a party in Cherry Hill, N.J, and the girl was there. I was dancing, and she came over and started trash-talking me. She heard that we were getting married and asked me when the baby was due, implying the reason we were getting married was because I was pregnant. She may very well have been right.

I had been pregnant, and that's when Alex said we should get married. We were already engaged since he proposed the previous Christmas with a ring. The proposal was in response to my mother throwing all my clothes out of my second-floor front bedroom window one night because I came home a little late. We got engaged but were leaving it that way for a while. Then I got pregnant, so we leveled up. Oddly enough, I had two miscarriages. I had been pregnant with twins and had one miscarriage. Then a few weeks later, I had another miscarriage. At that point, I told Alex we shouldn't get married anymore. But he said he still wanted to go through with our plans. Perhaps he was just being kind at the time.

Now you know the backstory to my night in Cherry Hill. This girl was dancing and swinging her hair into my face and antagonizing me, so I decided to fix her ass. I chewed a big wad of gum and pushed it deep into her long blond hair as close to her scalp as I could so that she'd have to cut her hair to get the gum out. When she realized what I did, she chased me outside into the parking lot and was ready to really brawl. Alex's brother and friends ran out and made sure the situation didn't spiral out of control. They were working the event, and it wouldn't have looked very professional with these girls fighting over the DJ.

That girl, I'll call her "Maria," seemed to be out of the mix for a few years. When my baby came along, I truly believed that my ex suffered from the Madonna Complex. Once he witnessed me give birth to our baby – arguably a scene for the records – our intimate relationship became almost non-existent. He was out there again with Maria. During this time, he would use the cover story that he was going "fishing" with a buddy a lot. Going on weekend fishing trips or wrestling events with his "work" friend. One day he said he wanted to take Alex with him to meet his buddy. I thought that was odd, but I capitulated. When my baby came home that day, he had long blond hair wrapped up in his chubby little fist, and I immediately knew what was going on.

A very big throwdown ensued. Alex was still involved with drugs at this point, but I was holding firm to a promise I made to GOD not to do drugs anymore. We had a fistfight that went from one end of the house to the other. We were beating the shit out of one another, literally. As I look back at that scene in my mind's eye, I'm proud of myself. My true grit came out that day, as it did one time many years ago in high school. It was like I was saying, "OH NO! You don't get to do this to me." And I meant it with everything I had inside me.

When I met Alex, I really fell for him. It was love at first sight. He was exciting and fun to be with. He made me feel special. He was older and had a better game with girls than the boys that I was used to dealing with. He was charming and would bring me flowers. He was an electrician with a very active side business as a DJ with a complete light show that he built himself using his electrician skills. He was hired to work parties most weekends and it was exciting. We would spend our weeknights picking up records from a new release club and spend time together categorizing or "timing" them. He taught me how to help him do this by finding the base beat and clicking a counter. It was so much fun at the time. The music was so loud; the whole house would vibrate, and his mom or dad would come down and have us lower it. It was as if I had fallen into my dream life. We were dressing for the club scene every weekend, and it was exciting. We were out there dancing all night at his gigs or going to the Rooftop and other clubs in New York City. For me, this was leveling up with what I already loved to do at this time in my life, and still do – dance. Now, listening to freestyle classics driving in the car with Anthony is my idea of an exciting night out. The years have robbed my ability to dance for five straight hours.

Before I knew Alex, I was already very into the dance club scene, at age sixteen, getting into the Showboat, Runners, Bayside 21, and Foxes – the name seeming to foreshadow my life from the jokes with Terri. Out dancing all night at sixteen was ridiculous. The cover story was that I was sleeping over at Michelle's.

Landing a handsome boyfriend who was a DJ by night and an electrician by day went with my vision of who I wanted to be at the time.

It was a second chance for a more mature relationship after Michael broke my heart by allowing his friends to treat me so badly. I'll never forget how hard I cried the day two of his friends came to my house and asked me to have sex with them. They said Michael said it was OK. I remember standing there in shock at what was being said to me. This is still something that I honestly can't believe happened. I also think it set the stage for the schoolyard guys to think they could get away with terrorizing me the way they did the day Larry Gannon came by and rescued me. Considering that I didn't agree to do anything with Michael for so long, I don't see how any of them thought this to be a reasonable plan. As I stood there in shock, crying on my porch, my heart literally died that day. It was dead for a very long time after that.

I dated to spite him and went out with other people, but it was all a cover for my broken heart. That was the end of my relationship with Michael. We broke up that day for good because of the following spill off, and for many years, had a back-and-forth volley that never was able to sync up again. All this because Michael sent them to ask me to do stuff with them so that he'd have an excuse to break up with me, either way, if I did or didn't. It was really all in very poor taste, even for an eighteen-year-old guy. It seemed below Michael to come up with this ridiculous plan so that he could go and do what he wanted with another girl without feeling bad. It just shows, though. We waited until our two-year anniversary, but once I finally agreed, believing his promises, it was on to greener pastures.

It was a poor plan; indeed, that really backfired. I went right out that night, because I always respond fast, and started talking to another guy, a football player from high school, who later got himself in some trouble, but it was only for a very short time, specifically to get back at Michael. Michael always held that he never came back to make up with me because of this guy. This seemed to be an illogical analysis of the situation, considering what he and his friends hatched up to get him some time off from me. He really expected me to just forgive this transgression just like that. Either way, the heartache was to follow because of my low self-worth. I should have never spoken to any of them ever again after that day, but I had to wait for the incident in the schoolyard to make my final exit.

This all happened right before I met Vinnie, who was one the nicest guys besides Anthony that I've been involved with. He never did a mean thing to me the entire time I knew him.

It was all very immature at the time, but I didn't realize what was really happening until later when I put all the pieces of the puzzle together. I was also shocked and devastated that Michael had an intimate relationship with another girl very quickly. – especially since we were each other's "first" and I had been putting him off for two years.

It was all just heartbreaking for me at the time. This also reinforced my feelings of being less worthy that I had always been trying to conquer. I thought I had finally found someone who saw who I really could be. A wild coincidence is that this girl is connected by marriage to Anthony. When I started dating Anthony, his aunt and cousins didn't care for me because of my past with Michael. Ten years later, I was still explaining my relationship with him to people.

The whole situation was really ridiculous, but my self-esteem took a big hit with Michael. When I met Alex, I wasn't as self-assured as I appeared on the outside. At the beginning of our relationship, Alex talked a lot about a girl he used to date, Dorothy. There was a night when I told him that I didn't want to see him anymore and felt he should go back to Dorothy because he seemed to still have feelings for her. At this point, I was purposefully trying to steer myself away from relationships that had red flags. I asked him to take me home that night after I talked with him very seriously. He then insisted on how wrong I was and that he was really taken with me and wanted to get to know me better. What actually happened was that I gave him a challenge. After knowing Alex over the years, once I trusted him and settled in, letting my guard down and taking away the challenge, it set the stage for what would follow after the initial romance had died down. Alex was onto other things as well. There was always too much work involved for me in relationships. I was also looking for more serious relationships because I wasn't going to just sleep around. I would always have to give up something that I didn't want to, my honor, my courage, or my pride, once they had me where they wanted me. This intensified the feeling that I didn't want to be humble unless it was on my terms. I will humble myself, but I won't allow others to humble me; it came off as a huge chip on my shoulder for many years. Only GOD would have that power over me. Finding this and being able to say it and act on it has released me from being a person who is taken advantage of and has given me the ability to become who I was meant to be.

The girl I wanted to be was always there, but I had to find the courage to bring her out. Being pushed back for so long made it hard, but that gritty nature of mine was boiling up in freshman year. There was a girl I had gym with, and her name was Rená as well. She called me out one day in the gym locker room, talking loudly to me, "You got eye problems?!?" – apparently wanting to instigate a fight. She more or less said if I didn't stop looking at her, she was going to kick my ass. For the record, I guess I did have eye problems; I heard this more than once when I was young. I wasn't staring at anyone, but I would go into a brain fog or freeze and stare into space at times. I was just taking a rest from the social anxiety. It was my way of shutting down or going radio silent for a minute, if you will. It made me a good target. I was definitely a bit gritty, and I had accumulated a big chip on my shoulder after the bullshit that I endured during grammar school. She thought she'd beat me easily or that I'd just back down. I remember thinking to myself at that moment in the locker room, "This is your time to prove yourself and not let what happened to you in grammar school repeat itself in high school." So I told her, "Yeah, maybe I do." I said, "Meet me under the bridge after school if you want to fight." She didn't show up after school, so I walked up to catch the bus on the Boulevard with my "friends." I think they came because the word got out that I may be in a fight after school. We were waiting for the bus, and when the bus came, my friends all got onto the bus before me. As I was stepping up onto the first step of the bus, Rená came up from behind and clotheslined me. I fell backward and slipped because it had just started snowing, and there was a light coating on the ground. Turning to see if my friends were going to get off the bus and help me, they didn't. I was standing there alone. We ended up having a pretty nasty fight on the Boulevard and 28th Street. I'll never forget taking off my fluffy soft mittens and throwing them to the ground because I knew I wouldn't be able to do any damage with those mittens on my hands. She was taller than me and had a longer reach, but I kept fighting her and getting up each time she knocked me down because the ground was so slippery. At the end of that fight, I got up, and she just stopped fighting me and said, "You surprised me." After that day, we were friendly toward each other; apparently, I had earned Rená's respect and the respect of her friends. That was a big day for me because that was the end of the days when I was picked on at school. From that point on, no one messed with me any longer in the locker room when we had to change for gym or in the halls of the school, for that matter. I had a little bit of notoriety as being tough. I wouldn't call it tough, but I definitely possess tenacity and grit.

You may be wondering what this has to do with being kind and learning from your experiences, and using your experiences to be empathetic in your interactions with the people that come into your life. This time it's to be kind to yourself, and there comes a point when you have to stand up for yourself and rewrite that narrative that has been written about you for too long. This moment was one of those rewrites for me. That day was on the calendar to revise and edit. I showed myself and my "friends," who stayed on the bus and kept going home that I wasn't going to allow people to intimidate me anymore. I proudly went into the store where we would meet up sometimes and let them all know that I had persevered. I wasn't someone to be counted out or overlooked. There was more there simmering than anyone suspected. But a shift was made. I would make my own mistakes, but I wasn't going to let anyone's opinion of me stop me anymore.

Circling back to the fight with Alex that went from the front to the back of the apartment because of the blond hair in my baby's little clenched fist. To help set the stage, my ex was a boxer, but I was so revved up on adRenáline that I was holding my own fighting him. He may have been holding back a bit, but honestly, I don't think so. When I told my son, Alex, this story, he said, "Mom, if he wanted to hurt you, he would have, believe me." I understand what my son was saying, and he is probably right, but at that moment that day, I gave it all I had. He had come in and gone to sleep, and I woke him out of a dead sleep to start fighting with him about the blond hair. I also think he was sleeping off a strong buzz, and he was really startled when I woke him to confront him. We broke everything in the house that day from one end to the apartment to the other. He even punched his hand and forearm through the front window and needed many stitches. That was what brought the commotion to an end. It was like something from a movie scene. I left there that day and never expected to ever go back or to be with him again. I called my parents and they came and helped me take some things I would need for Alex and I moved back home with my parents at that point.

A few months before that, we were having a good time, and I was participating in things that I shouldn't have been doing. Regretting any of my experiences would be a mistake because all of these experiences enabled me to understand and empathize with how people struggling with addiction survive and to the depths of despair drug addiction can bring you. I saw things up close and personal and even experienced addiction myself.

I had to go through withdrawal from Crack on my own because rehab was not possible for me at the time. With a heartfelt prayer to GOD on my knees, with a wet towel rolled up against my baby's bedroom door to make sure that the smoke from the pipe would not go into his room, I asked GOD to take my addiction from me, and GOD answered my prayer. The next day I woke up completely free from wanting anything to do with what I had become so addicted to. I had come to a point where I was literally crawling around on the floor, looking for any rocks that may have fallen. That was the moment when I saw myself and just stopped. I started really sobbing, sitting there on my kitchen floor alone. I promised GOD I would never do drugs again if HE would just take this addiction away from me and give me another chance. I have kept that promise ever since except for a few puffs of pot, or a couple of edibles, all totaling maybe five, over the last thirty-five years.

Medications and drugs have always affected me more than the average person. I have extreme reactions to certain prescriptions and almost died one night when I took Amoxicillin by accident. My first date with Anthony was cut short because I was feeling very sick. When I came home, my mom gave me amoxicillin, not realizing that I had developed an allergy to penicillin after I had left home. My dad had to rush me to the emergency room after my sister, Dena, alerted him that I was in bed gasping for breath and couldn't breathe. After the doctor gave me the Epipen and asked me how I was given a prescription, I said my mom had given it to me. The doctor asked me sarcastically what medical school my mother went to, and I told him the "School of Doctor Spock." The doctor thought that was funny and laughed, but I was serious. My mom always talked about how she got all her information regarding child care from this book because she didn't have a mom to ask childcare questions.

Knowing that I am very sensitive to certain foods and have had many reactions to prescription medications, I should have realized why I was feeling very strange while trying to quit smoking with the help of a prescription drug, Chantix. This medication literally made me crazy and gave me superhuman strength. The wall-to-wall rugs in my house needed to be removed because our dog, Honey, had far too many accidents on them, and we were planning to install laminate flooring. One night I decided to remove the carpet from the living room, which was pieced into two sections. It is a large room for a city house, maybe twenty feet by sixteen feet. I rolled the two pieces up and dragged them through my house, through the hall, down nineteen steps, and out to the front of the house, probably a thirty-foot distance to the front door from the staircase to drag them. I wanted to get it done that night because there was garbage collection around six-thirty the next morning. I was up all night by the time I had finished dragging them to the sidewalk. Knowing that the garbage truck would come, I waited. When the truck came down my block, they kept going and were about five houses past mine. Instinctively, I picked up this heavy roll of carpet. I'm not sure how heavy it was, but it must have been at least a hundred pounds. I picked it up as if I was lifting a barbell, and started running and simultaneously screaming at the guys to stop. When they did, both guys' mouths dropped open, their eyes expressing shock and total disbelief at what they were seeing. I ran up to the truck and threw the roll of carpet in and told them I have another and to wait. They watched me begin to run back for the other roll, and then yelled to the driver to back the truck up the block. They proceeded to take the second roll from the sidewalk while staring at me as if I was an alien coming out of a UFO.

It all started very casually for me. Going dancing in New York City at the Rooftop in the mid-80s, Alex would give me a line or two of coke or give me a little to take into the bathroom. It wasn't too extensive, just dabbling for me. I really didn't know how much Alex was doing at the time. He would give me a little here and there at different parties, and I liked the feeling of being hyped up and would dance all night long. That was really what I loved to do back then. Freestyle disco music and partner hustling were what I loved. For me, it was completely recreational at the time. Alex was dealing with something more. At our wedding, it was still just an add-on activity that didn't mean that much to me. To enhance our wedding reception, Alex gave me an envelope with more coke in it than normal. He told me to have fun and share it with my girlfriends in the bathroom. As I was setting the lines up in the bathroom on the toilet paper holder, I turned around, and the bow on the back of my wedding dress knocked the envelope – and everything I had set up on the top of the toilet paper holder – onto the wet floor. At that point, I wasn't too worried about it and told Alex what happened. He wasn't too upset but told me it was a lot of money that just went down the drain and proceeded to share a little more of his stash with me. As I was dancing to Madonna's "Like a Virgin" at my wedding, just eighteen years old, that was really the last worry on my mind.

Time marched on, and I would do a few lines with Alex here and there at night in our apartment on Zabriskie Street in Jersey City. We had all the amenities you could possibly imagine. Pot plants in the windows, an EZ wider dispenser on the bedroom wall as a decoration, and a couch in our living room that we unbolted out of Alex's van and used to furnish our apartment. We really thought it looked great. I had walked down to Rosen's on Central Avenue and bought two small fifteen-inch round glass and brass end tables to put on each side of the van couch. I stood back and thought it looked amazing. We had a three-shelf wood TV stand with a TV and VCR. Whenever I think back to that moment, I always shake my head and laugh at myself. That apartment was really something, I remember one day going into the bathroom, and there were hundreds of tiny baby roaches that somehow had hatched in the tub. My parents would come to visit and I would try to nonchalantly swat at roaches on the wall behind them before they would see them. I'm pretty sure they saw them but didn't say anything. When I look back, it was really terrible, but I was actually happy there at the time. That was the apartment where Alex was conceived. When I was about seven months pregnant, we moved into the upstairs apartment of his parents' two-family house on Summit Avenue. During my pregnancy, I didn't participate in drugs at all. I didn't drink coffee or alcohol or smoke cigarettes. During that time, Alex Sr. was devoted to me and the pregnancy. That was probably one of the best periods of our time together. We went on a camping trip to Lake George right before Alex was due. We rented a small boat with an outboard motor and went out on the lake. As it was getting dark, I could see that Alex didn't know how to get us back, but kept telling me he knew the way to keep me calm. He ended up hitting the propellers of the motor on rocks as we approached the shore. At this point, we were in the dark and couldn't see where we were going. As we walked up the steep incline from the boat to our campsite, I could feel the stretch marks ripping the skin on my lower abdomen. That was one of our best times overall. We were both happily awaiting our baby to be born.

The scene in the delivery room was another story. Alex was punching the walls in the delivery room because he felt I wasn't being properly attended to. He was right, but he could have kept himself calmer. The staff had me completely naked lying on the delivery table, with no sheet in sight for privacy. I repeatedly asked for a sheet because I felt overly exposed, and after several requests went unanswered, Alex lost it. They had to remove him from the room for a while until he promised to calm down. We were both a mess.

As always, Alex had a mind of his own, and he was three weeks late. The night before he was born, I shared a pot of coffee with my friend Michelle, who told me the coffee would get the baby moving. She was right. After I gave birth, I asked for a cigarette as the doctor was stitching me up in the delivery room, and they gave it to me easily. That was the best cigarette of my life.

After Alex witnessed me give birth, his attraction to me shifted to more of his baby's mother and less about us. He was very caring and attentive in helping me care for my post-delivery issues. Looking back, that may have been where the switch flipped in his mind. After we were about six months into being parents, he started going out more. Trying to keep him around, I would agree to party with him in the house at night after the baby was asleep. It started out as usual, just doing some lines. I would snort coke or even heroin at times, depending on what Alex had brought home. I never used needles, not once. My ex always told me he'd never let me do that, but even more than that, my extreme fear of needles most likely saved my life. After a few weeks, we moved into freebasing, and my ex would cook up the coke and we would smoke it. At least that's what he told me we were doing. I was never involved in the purchases; he would always go out to "cop" and come back home, sometimes. When he'd come back, I'd partake with him, at first because I was trying to keep him at home with me and to hold our connection together. But that caught up with me. After some time, when money was tighter, he would bring home vials with little white rocks inside that we would smoke the same way we would freebase. That's when the crack crept in, and the addiction really took hold of me. It was all I could think about during the day, waiting for him to come home so that we could smoke after we put the baby down for the night.

Shortly after my prayer to GOD to cure my addiction and the blond hair showing up in my baby's hand, I was faced with another very frightening experience – a waiting period to find out if I had HIV.

Even worse, our baby could also have been exposed through the pregnancy. I had to wait several weeks for the test to come back. I was living with my parents and believed that my marriage with Alex's dad was over. Michael was home on leave for a few weeks, and we were spending time together. As he was getting ready to go back to Washington, he told me he wanted to get back together and that he would be there to help me raise Alex. He invited me to move to Washington State, where he was stationed in the Air Force, and pick up where we left off. I was all in and very excited. It meant a lot to me at the time because I knew I wasn't making it all up in my mind about our past. Michael really did care about me. We had talked about the past and most of the things that had happened, except for the incident in the schoolyard when Larry came by as I was getting a "wedgie." I was still too embarrassed to talk about that incident to anyone. I also didn't want to start up any major drama at that time. We discussed the day on the porch with his two friends telling me he said it was okay to have sex with me was only a joke and that running out that night and meeting up with the football player made matters worse. Who knows? We were ready to move on and start a new life together. I'll always remember one particular day when we went to the mall, and he had Alex on his shoulders as we were walking around. He was really going to help me pick up the pieces of my life. Then I received a life-changing phone call that I had to be tested for HIV. I should have told Michael what was going on at this point, but I was too scared to tell him the truth. As all of this was happening, Yaya and Papou were pushing me to move to Pennsylvania with Alex and to give him another chance by removing him from his familiar surroundings. At that time, if it wasn't for all this, Alex and I would not have continued on. We were really done at this point. In the '80s, HIV test results took several weeks to come back. But I was negative, and so was our baby.

Giving Alex credit for not leaving me high and dry when I was pregnant in the beginning, I didn't feel it would be right to leave him at this point, just getting out of rehab with all these issues and fears to deal with. I felt like I would be leaving someone when they were down and at their lowest point, and I couldn't live with myself if I did that.

So, I wrote Michael a letter telling him I was going to stay with Alex, but I never explained why or what was going on. Michael never understood why I made this decision and he avoided even speaking to me for a few years. He also didn't know the whole story, and that I tested negative and knew that he never had anything to worry about, so I decided to just leave it alone. It's understandable that Michael was really mad at me, considering all the lead-up to the extremely difficult situation that I found myself in.

My memories have often been revisited by the night before my wedding when Michael came over to my parent's house and told me I shouldn't go through with it. I couldn't help thinking about my Grandparents Jessie and Jake and the similar events unfolding. The fact that they raised my dad and uncle in the same apartment where Michael and his family lived is a strange coincidence and I can't deny I thought it was some type of sign that we belonged together. However, he waited too long. So much had already happened between us. He had left me flat in the past, and the wedding was all set. Alex had just left my house when Michael rang the bell. I guess Alex came back around or was watching to see who might come by from across the street. What I do know is that there was some drama between Michael and Alex on 53rd Street the night before the wedding. From what I was told, Michael spent the day of my wedding at the bar, the next day, he joined the Air Force. Fast forward to this new crossroad with Alex. I really felt the right thing to do – considering all the circumstances – was to be there and support Alex. So that's what I did until he showed me that he still wasn't ready to stop.

I really wanted my marriage with Alex to work out. The day we got married, I really loved him and went into it thinking this would be forever. But I knew from day one it wasn't going to work. I bought Alex a gift on the morning of our wedding. It was a small charm that said "#1 Husband." I gave it to him after the ceremony in the limo, and when he opened it, he said, "I'm not going to wear this." Right there, I knew. I loved the fact that he wanted to get married to me, but I also knew that he had a wandering eye, but I hoped that being married would stop that. If he had been reasonably faithful to me, I think we'd still be married today. One or two small infractions could have been forgiven, but that wasn't in the cards. If all the cheating didn't happen, I would have stayed with him through the difficult times. But his cheating caused me to cheat, and that's what really ruined the marriage. After I found out that he'd been cheating on me with Maria, it really ruined it for me. I knew that he had other girls interested in him at work. One night I was cleaning out his lunchbox and found a note or "invitation to meet" slipped in by an admirer. The bottom line is Alex loved me but wasn't ready to settle down. Once I realized that, I decided I wasn't going to live that way. The marriage was doomed before we even began.

There was one time when we were participating in a study at Princeton University to research why I didn't contract HIV. The interviewer asked me if we had an open marriage and I remember feeling shocked at the question. It dawned on me that because I told the interviewer about my encounter with Michael that Alex must have recounted all his shenanigans. As a result, the interviewer thought we had an open marriage agreement. It was really a toxic situation, and I realized it then.

All these things were the simmering pot for much more. Having had this scare, people treated me differently, not wanting to be around me or my baby. Scared to touch me, kiss my cheek, shake my hand, and so on. This was what was going on at the time, and I experienced firsthand how people with infectious diseases feel when they are looked at and treated as if they are lepers. It was another hurtful time in my life. However, the gift was I learned to have empathy for people in these types of situations and have never felt scared to hold someone's hand who needed support, or look into the eyes of someone who came into my focus through work or in my personal life who I knew damn well was struggling with drug addiction and was having a hard time getting it together. Having been there has given me a war chest of empathy for many situations that I know is what GOD wanted me to have to do the work he had planned for me. That's why I was brought through all these experiences and saved by GOD alone so that I can have a truly empathetic heart for a wide variety of situations.

During my late teens and early twenties, I had the opportunity to visit the homes of people who literally were living with a five-gallon paint bucket in the middle of their living room where their children would urinate and defecate. Probably because something was wrong with their plumbing, but with a little more planning, a more discrete solution could have been put in place. There were some really very obscene environments that I witnessed firsthand.

A friend I met while working for Morgan Guarantee right after high school lived in a very large housing project in the Bronx. We ate lunch together every day at work, so when she invited me to come to stay with her for the weekend, I accepted. On the subway traveling to her apartment, I realized I was entering new territory. I was really scared and uncomfortable at what I was witnessing on the train. When I walked into her apartment, I had never been in a situation before where I was actually scared to sit down. Her family was very welcoming and offered me different foods that they had prepared. I was hungry but couldn't bring myself to eat much of anything. I accepted a plate to be polite and nibbled at it, but I was actually scared to eat because the number of roaches everywhere made me convinced that there had to be roaches in the food. Roaches were everywhere, crawling on the counters and the table. When it was time to go to sleep, and the lights were shut off, the roaches were literally crawling on me. They were in my hair and running up my shirt, and I felt them on the skin of my back. I couldn't stay; there was no way that I could sleep there. This family went out of their way to make me as comfortable as they could. They gave me a pillow and blanket to sleep on the couch. It was late, and it was dark. I left without saying goodbye to my friend because she was in a room with other people sleeping, and this was long before cell phones. I took the elevator down probably twenty or thirty floors, and left, walking through the neighborhood, asking people for directions back to the subway. I found my way and was robbed of my jewelry on the train that night by three guys that weren't too strong but saw a weak target. I was lucky that's all that happened to me. I was pushed around a bit but fought back because I always had that gritty nature. I had my high school ring, an "R" ring, and a few 14K gold necklaces with a cross and drama charms stolen, but I thankfully ended up with only a bruised face. After being lost on the subway for hours that night, getting on and off different trains, I found my way back to the PATH trains and, ultimately, Journal Square. That was another one of the scariest nights of my life.

There was another family that Alex and I would visit who had a ferocious dog tethered to a radiator with a very heavy chain. The dog was there most of the day, and when someone came into the apartment, he would viciously bark the entire visit and salivate when babies and young children were close by. The dog appeared to be trying to pull the radiator out of the floor to bite my arm off.

There were about ten feet between the couch and this dog pulling at the radiator. Between the five-gallon bucket scene and visiting with people who were living under the types of conditions I've described, all this seared an immensely impactful impression on me. I knew this wasn't the way I wanted to live and started to think seriously about how I would make sure that this didn't happen to me or my children. Ideas about getting an education started simmering in my mind at this point.

The different families I am reminiscing about all were friendly, hospitable, warm hosts who welcomed me into their homes. They wanted peace in their lives and to have enough money to provide themselves and their children with their basic needs and hopefully a little more. Their methods of getting the money they absolutely needed were sketchy because their options were limited. They all were kind-hearted people with children that they worried about and loved for sure. Jose, the guy with the dog, was a really good friend of my ex. They used to DJ together, and Jose would do anything for Alex. He worked really hard, putting in many hours of timing records and practicing the smoothest mixes back in the '80s. and he was an amazing DJ. At his apartment, he would always ask me if I wanted something to eat or drink. Being with people who live in this type of environment gave me a window into a way of life and a level of poverty that I would not know or understand if I hadn't met and spent time with these families. Again, all part of my education to understand more deeply what some of my future students and their parents were dealing with at home.

Everything is relative to your own experiences. I believed I had grown up poor, but this was a different type of poverty that I was seeing firsthand. It seemed to include poverty of expectation. One thing I know is that almost every parent wants to see their children safe and well. They may deliver it differently, but everyone, every human being on the planet, wants the same thing. As Maslow's hierarchy states, to have your basic needs met, to belong to a group, to feel safe, accepted, and loved. When one or more of these things are missing, there is something lost from that person, which makes them not whole. *For me, feeling accepted for who I knew I was, was always missing.* If you can't find it among the people you are around, you will go find it somewhere else. That's the doorway for danger to enter a young person's life and why many young people enter gang life. This is why I want anyone who reads this book to take away that just being kind to someone can change everything for them. These feelings were internalized, and that's why I needed to come to a final boiling point and rewrite my own narrative.

Kindness can help address basic needs. Many students are suffering from food insecurity, and feeling unsafe, not accepted, understood, or loved. Small actions such as being present, making eye contact, and showing a young person that you care. Greeting them in a welcoming way, as if they are visitors to your home.

Offering a light snack to give them the calmness they need to settle in and focus. One person will never know what another person is going through, has gone through, or is currently dealing with. When you realize and acknowledge this, it's easier to give people, particularly children, more leeway.

People in trouble need someone to look at them and truly see them. To see their heart and their pain and acknowledge their circumstance. Let them know, you are aware, *they have obstacles to overcome for themselves before they can help their children.* If you can show this compassion or humanity in your heart to someone at that moment, you have a chance to reach this person and help shed light on what they need to do and make the decision to shift gears.

Give someone a phone number of an agency that can help. Invite them to sit with you for a few minutes while you look up some resources on the spot and print them or write it down for them. The odds are, if you let them leave that moment without something tangible in hand to do as a first step, no movement will be made. Giving that person a first step, a way, a chance, will put hope back into their thoughts. It costs the giver of hope nothing. *"The journey of a thousand miles begins with one step," said Chinese philosopher Lao Tzu.*

Inertia can be a friend or foe. Give a student's parent or guardian your phone number and tell them you will give them a ride somewhere if they need it. Offer your time to them when it's convenient for them. These small offerings of support can be a huge hand up and out for some people who are stuck in their situation and inertia has a grip on them. Once you get someone moving, then the inertia will keep them moving. It's that initial push into motion that makes all the difference.

Having been there – "in it" – with people struggling like this was eye-opening to me. Whether visiting a friend or "copping" some drugs, I've seen a spectrum of lives up close and understood that even though things looked really bad on the outside, all these people had the potential to do much better. This window into people's lives would later enable me to show empathy, kindness, and compassion. I knew these people loved, worried, and cared about their children and were looking for a way to help their children but didn't know how to make it happen because no one ever showed them how it was possible. Or they never knew or actually witnessed someone in their own family or extended friend group accomplish upward mobility through hard work and/or education.

Drug addiction and poverty will do crazy things to your judgment and how you live your life. I've seen it and experienced it. When I see someone I think is dealing with this, I don't run away. I'll talk to them, give them hope, tell them about my own experiences, if I can, or at least that I understand, and express that there is a way out if you can just believe in yourself and in GOD to help you. Call on GOD with a broken and open heart, and HE will come. If you truly want to break the cycle, it can be done. I did it all on my own, but I had examples of successful role models along the way that made a difference. I've seen many people make it through education and/or hard work: my parents, my friends' parents, Alex's parents, and Anthony's parents. I believe GOD made sure that he could work through me to turnkey others along the way.

Many more experiences were added to my war chest at this time in my life. Alex's parents, who had far more financial resources than mine, gave us a down payment for a house in the Poconos. We moved there to remove Alex from familiar routines, people, places, and things, and we lived there for about a year and a half. But the drug problem kept creeping back in, and he would ask me to have sex without a condom. That was like playing Russian Roulette to me and helped me lose any feelings of loyalty that were holding me to him. There has been a recurring theme in my life – people who were supposed to be close to me, asking very outrageous things of me. On top of all this, I was a city girl and was not apt at keeping the house warm with a wood-burning stove or having to deal with a septic tank's leach field that would back up. There were a lot of problems including heavy snow and icy weather. I was alone with a toddler in this Poconos house often because Alex was still functioning as a magnet to Jersey City and his bad habits. The final straw was when he didn't come home one Christmas Eve until almost six in the morning, and we had both of our families coming for the holiday. I remember being up all night worried that Alex would wake up Christmas morning and his dad wouldn't be there. That night I decided that no matter what, I couldn't do this anymore.

I had enrolled in Northampton County Community College at this time and was taking classes. I knew if I wanted to leave Alex, I had to get a job, and I did. I found an apartment closer to where I worked, and I moved out one morning after Alex left for work – a few months after my Christmas Eve decision. Of course, it couldn't be an amicable separation. Looking at all that had happened and was still going on, it just wasn't working. It turned into a very nasty custody fight of our son. There were a lot of lies told, such as I was a drunk driver and didn't have locks on my car doors. At that point in my life, I rarely ever drank, and my car surely had locks. With his parents' help, Alex retained a highly regarded custody attorney in Pennsylvania, and gained full custody of Alex for approximately a year. I was beside myself with grief and anger during this time. I never brought up or used my ex's health condition to prove my side of the story in the court proceedings. I felt like that was off limits and unfair. I could barely think because I was so distraught and stricken with sadness and fury at the same time, because Alex wasn't with me every day. I only had him with me from Friday after school until Monday morning, but that didn't feel right.

After some time, I moved back to New Jersey because I had now met Anthony, and we were getting more serious. Alex was with his dad during the week, and I had an opportunity to upgrade my job at the time. I was now working for a law firm in Jersey City and would leave work at three in the afternoon on Fridays to drive to Stroudsburg in the Poconos to get Alex from daycare and then bring him back to Bayonne. We'd spend the weekend together, and on Monday, we would leave the house at five in the morning so that I could get him to daycare in the Poconos and drive back to Jersey City for work by nine o'clock. I did this for the entire time that he was with his father during the week. During this time, my son was told many lies, such as I left him because I didn't love or want him, I was the devil, and many other things that really confused him and injured his self-esteem as a small child. Alex actually asked my mother if I was the devil. He told her that was what Yaya told him. My mother explained as best she could that I wasn't the devil, but this is an example of the type of things my three-year-old son was being told about me, his mother. At that time, he had no idea how hard I was fighting to get him back.

I never had chickenpox as a child, and when I caught it from my son, I had a very bad case. The itchy welts were in my eyeballs and everywhere you could possibly imagine that would be painful. I was too sick to take care of Alex, so I asked Yaya to care for him while I recovered. Alex and his family took that opportunity to say that I abandoned my son. It was an utter lie, but that was what happened, and the opportunity was taken to go to court and say that I abandoned him; that's how the whole saga erupted.

It took many years to try to repair the damage that was done to Alex during this time. It will never be fully repaired. So many damaging experiences happened to both of us at this time. But when I come across parents who are dealing with these difficult custody situations, I empathize and show that I understand how difficult this situation can be for all involved – both the children and the parents. These years gave me a window into these situations and helped me to be a more understanding teacher because I'm able to empathize with some of the background problems which may be making the lives of parents and students more stressful and difficult to handle – in turn, causing the children anxiety, which hinders them from reaching their potential in the classroom. When children are separated from their mothers and fathers, it hurts them. Emotional wounds are harder to heal than physical ones.

It is a fact that when you are anxious and highly stressed, you cannot learn. An anxious person is in fight or flight mode, which makes learning new material impossible. To be able to focus, a student has to be at ease. Only in a calm state are you able to take in new knowledge, process that information into short-term memory, and later, when sleeping, process it into your long-term memory. When children come to school stressed and anxious and return home with more anxiety, this really puts them at a disadvantage in processing any information that they were exposed to during the day.

As a teacher, it is so important to be cognizant of how the brain processes new information, and when the brain can't process due to fear, anxiety, stress, or anything that makes a student feel unsafe and/or anxious, including being presented with work that is outside their zone of proximal development. Understanding that offering a sincere greeting as students walk into the classroom, providing a few crackers when they are feeling hungry, smiling while making eye contact, or giving a pat on the arm or back while working on something gives students hope and confidence that can make all the difference. Enabling a child to feel safe – for at least the duration they are in your class – is a way of showing kindness to those who may really need it. You may be the only purposefully kind person such a student comes in contact with all day.

When small children are told that one or both of their parents can't or won't take care of them, it is very damaging to their self-worth. Sarcastic teachers are another damaging factor at school. I've experienced sarcastic teachers as a student and know how hurtful this was to my learning process in their classes. Learning didn't happen because I didn't feel I was in a safe environment. At any moment, I could be the butt of their joke or called out to do something that would embarrass me in front of my peers. That worry alone will stop any stored learning from happening.

An educator has an opportunity to mitigate those feelings for a little time each day. That half hour to an hour can make the difference for students who just need a reprieve from anxiety. It is such a nice feeling to know you can be that safe space for them, at least for a little while on school days.

All these factors are on my mind when I am looking for reasons why a student may seem completely disengaged and shut down. It may not be the schoolwork, but social-emotional problems at home or in another class. Having had these types of problems myself, and with my own children, has given me another window into understanding many different students and the personal issues that are holding them back from engaging in their education in a meaningful way. Being able to talk to my students and share my various vignettes with them enabled me to help them understand that there may be issues going on behind the scenes with their parents that they do not understand or are unaware of.

Recognizing these types of problems and sharing stories from my past – particularly how I was separated from my son for a time, how that negatively impacted him, and how it hurt me – has helped a few students along the way understand that there may be more to the story than they understand at the moment. Giving their parents a chance to explain can help parents and their children heal from past experiences. Listening to the kids and parents and empathizing with many of their situations is something I wouldn't be able to do without all the negativity

I had to live through to build up this toolbox of mine. Because I truly empathize and understand that these situations are not easy to maneuver, I am kind and as helpful as I can be. Helping the parents in whatever way I can to try to work together for their child. Having been there makes it easier for me to recognize and help.

Anthony made sure that the very tough situation I was in came to an end before we were married. He borrowed five thousand dollars from his parents to help me get Alex back full-time. I needed the money to hire a top-notch attorney with a reputation for being a bulldog. Anthony researched and retained that attorney. Within a week of the attorney writing the "$5,000 letter," as we often reminisce, I was heading to meet my ex and Alex at the Texaco off Exit 45 on Route 80, to have my son returned back to my full custody. Aside from my mother, Anthony has always been my biggest supporter. He never gave up on me, even when I made it very difficult. Everyone needs someone who believes in them to help them. Anthony was the first person to truly have my back, no matter what, and he has maintained this throughout our entire life together.

After this very emotional and traumatizing time for both myself and Alex, we began to heal and readjust to our lives back together again without having to drive for eight hours each weekend to be together.

Years went by, and Anthony and I started a few different businesses. I always had the entrepreneurial bug. First, we had a hot dog cart and Italian ice cart, and later a lunch truck, "R&R's

Lunch Box." We started the lunch truck with what was left from our wedding money, after we paid back the five thousand dollars to his parents.

After we sold the truck, we moved up to a brick-and-mortar business, "Lighten-Up: The Healthy Way Cafe." It was a restaurant ahead of its time. No one was putting nutrition facts on their menus at that time. Everything was baked; no fried food. We made whole-wheat pizza and used low-fat cheeses. We used only chicken, turkey, and fish in our dishes; no beef.. I figured out the calories and fat content in all the recipes and had the serving size, calories, and nutritional facts on the menu back in 1997. It really was a nice little cafe, but the interest and foot traffic weren't there. In an attempt to save the business, we reopened it as "The Mess Hall." We worked hard, but the neighborhood wasn't ready for us yet. After pushing for about three years, we gave up.

During this time, my lifelong best friend, Dana, was there supporting me again. When we first opened "Lighten-Up," it had a lot of initial interest. We should have started with a soft opening, but weren't experienced or savvy enough at the time to know about these things. Dana has always had the right connections, and as she always does, she helped me out in real time. She arranged for a consultant to work with us to improve the flow of our kitchen and reduce the time it took to plate meals or package them for delivery. Dana was also there when Alex was a toddler and would drive to Pennsylvania to watch him when I had to go to Princeton

123

University to participate in the HIV study. While we would talk often, we could also go radio silent for months. But we will always pick up as if we spoke yesterday. We have had our fights and disagreements, but when the chips are down, we know we can count on each other to be there, front and center, as always.

Honestly, I believe that scare was just another one of the miracles that continue to happen to me throughout my life. All these situations are a tether that keeps me focused on the fact that my entire life has been predestined by GOD's plan for me and what I am expected to do with all these experiences. I truly believe HE is working through me and wants me to be a witness to it all. That's why I decided to share my incredible story of overcoming obstacles that many people living on the fringes experience, but don't see a way to overcome. I want readers to know that it is possible to become a kind, smart, and a valuable professional person, even if no one ever told you that was possible.

Chapter 10: Unexplainable Moments

After thirty years together, Anthony and I are comfortable financially, but we struggled when the kids were young. Between Alex, a tween, Jake, an infant, and the restaurant taking up all our time and energy, we were working around the clock and I didn't realize I was pregnant. I wasn't feeling well and suddenly, without warning, I miscarried and found out I was five months pregnant. This was after Jake but before Gia who are only twenty-three months apart.

It wasn't something that I ever paid too much attention to. We were really busy, so I just kept moving, and it was written off as something that happened. Anthony pondered on it and talked about it more than I did. It upset him more than me at the time. We didn't tell many people or make much of it.

A few years ago, my sister-in-law, Lisa, went to a medium. Through the medium, Lisa had a conversation with her dad, who passed away in 1993 a few weeks after our wedding. He told her a few things and then said that he watches over Anthony's little girl and holds her hand every day. She called to ask if I ever lost a baby and I told her what happened. After that talk with Lisa, and after telling Anthony about this, I decided I should give our baby girl a name, and I named her Mary in honor of the Blessed Mother.

When Gia was born, we were on public assistance, receiving WIC and Medicaid. Through my pregnancies with Jake and Gia, I went to the free clinic and my OB-GYN put me on a payment plan. We went through Bayonne Hospital's Charity Care program for the hospital bill. With both babies, I was admitted, gave birth, and released within twenty-four hours. When I was pregnant with Gia, at first, I went to the clinic but then went back to the doctor that delivered Jake. Sixteen weeks into the pregnancy, after a blood test, I was advised by the attending doctor at the clinic to have an abortion. He said, "This baby has Spina Bifida and will be a vegetable with no quality of life." After talking with Anthony and my mother, it was decided that we would deal with whatever we were given by GOD and Gia was born just fine. Gia was born with Spina Bifida, but the doctors did not tell me at the time that outcomes could vary. They told me only the worst-case scenario. Just because the testing showed that the baby's spinal cord was not fused at the end, depending on the severity of the gap, will dictate the level of disability. Yes, Gia has back issues and will struggle at times with pain, and they have been treated intermittently through the years by a chiropractor for adjustments. This is far removed from being a vegetable, as I was told our baby would be.

Because we were struggling financially with our business when Gia was less than a year old, I decided to take a chance and applied to the US Postal Service. I took the test and received a letter stating I could work for a trial period of ninety days. I accepted the job. We closed the doors of our restaurant permanently because we felt we needed the health benefits and financial security this position would provide our family. Anthony was working on the Mister Softee Truck in the spring and summer and driving a cab in the off-season, but it just wasn't enough to support everything pressing down on us.

We believed the mail carrier job was going to be the life change we were looking for. After the initial ninety days, I would be in the union and we'd finally have benefits. I was fired the evening of my eighty-ninth day. The reason, I was told, was that I didn't deliver the mail fast enough. Of course, that wasn't true. I had been doing a good job at keeping up with the men. But I was one of only two females at the Westfield location, and the other had just gone out on disability for a work-related injury. The people in charge didn't want to risk admitting another female into this particular post office.

One day, I was driving the mail truck around a circle in Westfield, going from one side of town to the other. I needed to get across several lanes so I could reach the turnaround, but there were too many cars going too fast, and I couldn't cut across. I was feeling overwhelmed, and time was beating down on my back with this job. The pressure to get to the next "Park and Loop" of my route. Seated on the right side of the vehicle, I felt like I was going to get forced onto an unfamiliar road, taking me off course, and making me fall behind schedule. It was a moment I felt I had nothing to lose. In the middle of all this moving traffic, I closed my eyes and called out, "Jesus help me." In that second, the mail truck was lifted up and placed over to the left so that I could reach the road I needed to be on. It was as if time stopped for a split second, and I was shifted over. I remember it happening. While I don't have any witnesses to back this up, I have no reason to lie or make things up, either. It really happened. That's why part of my story is about simply giving it up to the Universe – having belief in something that goes beyond this side of the world that can't easily be explained.

When I worked at the USPS, it felt like hazing. Each day I was assigned a different route, always heading into an unknown situation. Routes with heavy loads to carry on foot, or with nasty dogs that would chase me and bite at the back of my calves and heels. Each day I would come back within the time limits, then be given a more difficult route the next day, which had to be completed in the same amount of time. It was as if the supervisor was trying to purposely break me, but they didn't.

This was a completely devastating time for me. I had no idea what to do next or how to come back from this. We had decided to close our restaurant and sell the equipment based on my securing this position with steady income and health benefits, something we had not had up to this point. We had coverage for about a year while we had the restaurant, but it was costing more than we could pay, so we had to let it go. We had been going to Doctor Alonso on Avenue B in Bayonne. He would give Jake his vaccinations and ask us to pay what we could, which would be five or ten dollars at the time. He has passed on now, but he was a kind doctor who helped us and many people in need from the community. Once Gia came along, we applied for and were covered under Medicaid until I was hired as a teacher a few years down the road.

This was another one of those low periods in my life. After buying a car to get to and from the USPS job, I was completely dejected and broken. It took several weeks of soul searching – and a chance meeting with someone at the ShopRite deli counter – to figure out my next move. Renátta, who I knew from high school, told me she became a special education teacher and really enjoyed her job. She told me she worked with small groups with students who were similar to how "we" were in high school. A lightbulb went on in my head – one of the "ah ha" moments of my life. I thought to myself, she works with the "spicy kids"!

Chapter 11: Getting It Done

Within days, after talking with Anthony and my mom about my next move, I went to New Jersey City University and applied for admission to study and become a special education teacher. This was one of the best moves I have made in my life. I finally found my calling and what I was meant to do. It has been the toughest job of my life but completely the most rewarding. Each day I use moments from my past life when talking and working with my students and during discussions with their parents. As a special education teacher, I can use my empathy when I look back to being one of these children who was "lost in the sauce" in school. I can see myself as a parent of one of these students. On more occasions than I can count, I had been on the receiving end of a call from a teacher complaining about Alex's behavior. All these calls also went into my war chest of my experiences as a parent of a "spicy child" to talk with parents about their "spicy children." Having a cayenne pepper-level spicy child of my own has helped me dramatically during my career.

Alex taught me so many valuable lessons. The first time I knew I was in for some trouble with Alex, was when we were living in an apartment on 29th Street in Bayonne. Alex's first best friend, Dan, also lived on the block. They were about six years old, and I would allow him to ride his bike on the block with Dan. A neighbor knocked on my door and asked if I knew that Alex was playing "Chicken" in the middle of Avenue C with Dan. I ran to find him lying in the middle of the street, and screamed at him all the way home. He was always fearless but also very sensitive and hurt by all the inconsistencies surrounding his life at the time. He was a challenging teenager through no fault of his own. It was the mixed messages of the complicated co-parenting and grandparenting he was raised under. There was constant conflict and strife throughout his formative years. He was always a tough little guy. When he wasn't quite three, my mom and I took him to a park in Tannersville, PA. He joined some kids who were climbing a ladder that was enclosed in a steel tube, to reach a treehouse at the top and then come down the slide... He fell backwards and smashed his head on the steel lip that the kids had to step over to enter the tube. He was lying there for a few seconds while I rushed over to him. I had been in the front of the slide, waiting for him to get to the top and fire the pretend rifles attached to the treehouse. I picked him up and asked him if he was alright. Seeing how upset I was, he said, "Don't worry, Mommy, I'm alright." He just shook off the injury and wanted to keep playing. Looking back, I should have taken him to the hospital for a concussion check, but honestly, I didn't. He just wanted to keep playing, and he seemed alright, so that's what I let him do. Apparently, he was OK. He definitely is a true warrior, always has been and always will be.

Alex did many dangerous things. In sixth grade, he and some friends ran away heading for Canada, and they made it all the way to Rhode Island before being intercepted. He did this in response to my tremendous overreaction when he got into some trouble with a group of friends. My immediate response when he came home that day, after learning what transpired, was to hit him over the head with a frying pan – my Grandma Jessie's pan that was hanging on the wall as decorative memorabilia. He was knocked out for a few seconds then got right up. He still has a dent in his head from the force of that pan, and never misses an opportunity to bring it up when we visit. I scared him about what could happen to him as a consequence of the trouble he was in, and he felt he had no choice but to run away. It was very wrong on my part, and one of those times as a parent when I made a serious miscalculation. I am truly sorry that I reacted that way at that moment, but it was done, and I couldn't erase it. I was at my wit's end – out of ideas of how to corral him and his antics – and also worried that his dad would create drama by threatening to take him away from me again, which was always lurking in the back of my mind.

When I came home from work the next day, Alex had spray-painted a goodbye letter on his bedroom door – clearly letting me know how angry he was with me. From there, an Amber Alert was issued for him and his friends. To raise funds for the bus fare to Canada, I later learned he had pawned all of the memorabilia and valuables he had collected as gifts through the years, including his baseball cards and electric guitar. After he had been missing for over a day, we received a call that he and his friends were found walking on a highway in Rhode Island, trying to hitch a ride north.

Their funds had taken them as far as they could go. His father and I had to take the trip together to go get him and bring him home.

That was an interesting ride, for sure, each of us blaming the other. The ride home was even worse. When we walked into the Juvenile Center, he was eating McDonald's and seemed to be at ease. We had a lot of work ahead of us, but from there, things started to improve slowly. I did some great parenting with him and some awful parenting as well. There is a lesson to learn in all that as well. Never give up on your child, ever. And don't smash them in the head with a frying pan. I just thank GOD that he came out of it all strong, and not concussed, and driven to be a good man. Today, Alex is a husband, father of two, earned a master's degree in organizational leadership, graduated Summa Cum Laude, and is very successful in his chosen career. So I guess we all did a few things right too.

Seeing him grow up to be such a success also drove home the reality that the "spicy" kid in the class – the one most teachers wish would just stay home – can be a diamond in the rough who will do great things. When I started going to school for special education, Alex was already in his early teen years. At twelve, he was taking the train into New York City to play Warhammer at Neutral Ground, and has continued to play competitively since then. He would stay out until late at night, and I really had no way to monitor him since this was before cell phones. He was going to raves in New York City and missing in action a lot of the time. I would call Neutral Ground and ask if he was there. There were nights that he slept there with his friend Kyle, who remains his friend today. I would try to block him from going out by sitting directly in front of the front door, and he would just slide me out of the way. I started to use the strategies I was learning in school on him. His behavior fed my interest in learning about managing adolescent behaviors in my own home and in the classroom. It all worked together for me. I tried many strategies, some would work and some wouldn't. Alex gave me the business because, deep down, he believed I abandoned him. He worked at ShopRite during high school and became a head cashier. While shopping there one day, a woman started telling me how wonderful Alex was. I looked at her and asked, "My son, Alex?" and I gave his last name. She went on to tell me what a polite and diligent worker he was. Another time, when he was younger and still disappearing at night and coming home early in the morning, I used to volunteer to sit for adoration hours at St. Michael's Church. I was supposed to be there at five in the morning, and he had walked in right before I was supposed to go. I told him he had to go to the adoration for me because I had been up all night waiting for him and was too tired. I gave him a bag of rice and told him to kneel on it at church and say a prayer for forgiveness. When he came home, he told me he kneeled on the bag of rice for the entire hour because he thought that's what I wanted him to do. The person who relieved him told me they found him kneeling on the bag of rice, so I know he was telling me the truth. I didn't mean for him to kneel on it for the entire hour, but he did. These are the things that reassured me he was a very special and good person in his heart, but he was also very hurt by all the things that had happened to him as a small child. The harder the shell, the softer the filling, is a lesson I am reminded of when thinking of my son. Again, these are lessons I take with me into the classroom each day when trying to connect with my students.

Being patient and kind and letting him know that I loved him and that I cared about him and his future was always at the forefront of my mind. Particularly because I knew that he was very hurt and damaged by the period of time when we were separated when he was between three and four years old. I always knew that this had so much to do with all his behavior problems, and I always knew that hurt fueled his bad behavior.

Recognizing these feelings in the eyes of my students is a gift or skill acquired through life experiences. When I have students who are presenting this way, I have a window in. I'm able to help stitch up some of those wounds by explaining some of the things that happened in my own home. Giving them a way to understand what their parents may have been going through. I've had more than a few students who are struggling with feelings of abandonment by a parent; they may be in foster care or living with an adoptive parent. When a student infers or presents that this may be an issue for them, I will share my story of what happened in my own home and how my son and I were separated for a period of time, and how much it hurt him and me as well. I've explained how things happen in adult lives that they might not understand but that their parents do love them but may be caught in a situation, maybe something similar to what happened to me. When I tell a student about the time when my son and I were separated, they stop and listen. These hurtful lessons that are in my past are also part of my war chest of experiences that help me connect with my students and parents. Again, I've found a way to turn very negative experiences in my life into positives going forward. I've found that my most traumatizing and hurtful experiences are the ones that have been the most valuable in my classroom. They help me read the emotions of my students and share meaningful stories that can help them start to heal. For a child to have a window to start to talk about what happened, and to provide that student a theory or possible explanation of their parent's assumed lapse, can really raise that child's self-esteem. Once you can pick up a child's self-esteem, a more positive self-efficacy is likely to develop.

Another example of how my children have helped me be a better teacher is when Gia was in first grade and exhibiting a learning disability. I was in total denial. Not my child, I thought. I went to meet with the teacher, and Ms. Corcoran showed me examples of Gia's work. She showed me a paper with directions to draw three rectangles, and on the paper, there were three triangles drawn. I was indignant and started to get heated with the teacher because all I had seen was the "three." I said, "Yes, I see the three triangles. What's wrong with it?" I was getting very upset. This was my child, and my Mama Bear claws were up and ready to swipe in. The teacher stopped me and pointed at the word "rectangles." When she made me focus, I realized it was the shape that was wrong, not the number drawn.

I realized how emotional I was getting because I felt I was on the hot seat – being told my child wasn't up to snuff. I always remember that moment during hard meetings with my students' parents. I go back and remember how I felt when I was that parent sitting there. I wish Gia's teacher had handled the situation better with me, instead of putting me on the defensive. I always begin by telling the parents about the positives I see in their child. Being kind and showing you care about someone else's child is very important to a parent who is feeling their child is being put under a microscope.

Speaking with a parent of a "spicy" child, as my son Alex was, gives me repose. I am able to connect with that parent through my various experiences as a parent. I let them know I've been there too, and I understand. Being kind and sharing my truth has helped me over and over again. Not being too proud to admit that I've had troubles with my kids as well, and it can work out. Being humble enough to be vulnerable with parents is an important part of my teacher toolkit.

Jake was always a mild-mannered, soft-spoken little boy. Sweet-natured, patient, kind, polite, and highly intelligent, we were very surprised to be called to school for a meeting regarding

Jake's behavior in class. When my husband and I showed up, we were told how cranky and aggressive he was in school. Sitting there shocked and stumped, we looked at each other in surprise and said, "Our Jake, really, he's such a patient and gentle little boy?" After explaining the morning routine to Mrs. River and taking what we said into consideration said that she would try a few things with Jake based on our conversation. When she called us back in, she told us everything was better. After talking with us about Jake's morning routine, she discovered that, as we suspected, the reason for Jake's cranky behavior was because he wasn't getting breakfast at the babysitter's house. When she started offering him a bowl of cereal in the morning, everything changed immediately, and the Jake we described to Mrs. River returned to the class. This was an important lesson for me to bring forward and I always have small snacks available for hungry students. It is amazing what a few crackers, cookies, or a piece of gum can do to change a child's mood and make them feel cared for, comfortable, and at ease. This amazing teacher taught me a valuable lesson that I have used with hundreds of students in the last twenty-one years. Learning from negative situations is a powerful instrument to put in your own war chest of powerful combative techniques to fight off negative self-images. When a child in front of you feels cared about, there's a chance that you can raise their expectations for how they see themselves in the future. Kindness is such a simple way to make a big difference in our society.

Chapter 12: An Outline to Consider

Born in 1966 to moderately conservative parents who supported Nixon, read Steinbeck and Bronte, and listened to Simon and Garfunkel, Neil Diamond, and Willie Nelson, can give you a broad-stroked image of my background. My mother, a registered independent, despises Jane Fonda and considered herself a beatnik in her youth. She has always been talented artistically and tells of days when she cut class and went to Washington Square Park in New York City to simply sketch what she observed there. My Grandmother Dorothy wanted her girls to have careers. As I mentioned earlier, my grandma enrolled my mom in a drafting course at New Jersey Institute of Technology right after high school. After the first semester, she wouldn't allow her mom to re-enroll her. She worked at Macy's on 33rd Street in New York City and later completed a course to become a telephone operator. She had many different jobs, but once she became a mom, she decided to stay home.

My mother lost her mom, dad, and brother all by the time she was nineteen. This weighed heavily on her. As she was raising us as young children, she would go in and out of depressive states. Christmastime was especially tough for her, and thus, for us. At the time, I didn't understand what my mom was thinking about and experiencing. I was a typical egocentric child who only saw the world through my lens. It took me many years to understand the highs and lows of my mother's state of mind more clearly.

My parents cared for me and supplied me with my needs: a solid and clean home, dinner on the table. Extras were Christmas and birthday presents most of the time. My mom loved me very much and felt she had family again when I was born. I know she was doing the best she could, and I recognize that without my parents, I would have no story to tell. No mistakes to help me learn and grow.. Understanding that all of it – the good, the bad, and the ugly – was GOD's plan for me and my destiny is what I'm trying to drive home in this adventure I've undertaken. Mistakes were made so that I could have something to work on, improve upon, correct, and learn from – to bring it forward through helping others. Someone had to fail me so that I could learn a lesson to bring forward. This is what my life's purpose has been. I stand on the shoulders of my parents and the mistakes they made and also the other people who impacted my self-esteem and development, making me who I am today.

Mom would read Dr. Suess's books to me at night sometimes, but I knew she was skipping words because the spoken words didn't match the spaces between the words on the page. I still couldn't read, but the mismatch of text to words, or one-to-one match, didn't help my reading development. I needed what I was hearing and seeing to match up. I can remember sitting there watching, listening, and noticing that the words on the page didn't match the spoken words or groups of phonemes put together, and I was confused. I would have never put this together, but through my training to become a reading specialist, I studied the importance of pointing to each written word as it is read, in order to develop the one-to-one association of each spoken word, comprised of phonemes and morphemes, to each printed word or group of graphemes made me realize that this mismatch of written words to the spoken language most likely added to my reading deficits in understanding at a young age. This mistake was the foundation for reading problems that I would spend years overcoming, and likely prompted me to develop the skills to reach children and adults who struggle with their reading development. This was my destiny. It was my mother's destiny to make this mistake so that later, I would be able to reach many other people. As a past struggling reader, I am able to understand where the difficulties come into play and explain with experience and empathy to children and adults how to overcome reading problems with phonemic awareness, phonics, decoding, fluency, comprehension, and vocabulary development in a calm and empathetic way, filling in the gaps using my personal life experience.

One of my first memories, besides sitting on my Pop-Pop's lap in my grandparents' apartment, is having an explosive fit outside Hyman's Shoe Store at three years old because my mother wouldn't buy me the shoes I wanted. I threw myself into the street, kicking and screaming. The red Mary-Jane shoes with the tear drop design over the front were my shoes of choice. Mom felt I should continue to wear the sturdy lace-up white baby walkers. A few years later, hand-me-downs from my cousin, who was eight years older than me. Accordingly, I was wearing '60s outfits to school in the '70s. Kids can be cruel, and they were. This was how it all started. I was bullied, spit on, chased, and made fun of daily for most of my early years.

I felt helpless and hopeless at eight, nine, and ten years old. I was picked on in school to the point that I would lay in bed at night and cry, trying to figure out how I could end my life. This is the reason why I believe teaching kids to "Just Be Kind" is really important.

Bullying is a real struggle for many kids. My first best friend, Jill, and I were chased and called "10." Jill was and still is slim and athletic, so she was the "1." I was chubby and clumsy, so I was the "0." I think it was more traumatizing for me because I was the chubby one. Being slim was fine, but together we were prime targets. It was 1976. Bo Derek, who starred in the movie, "10," was famous for her sexy body, and the kids in our neighborhood had a good handle on the use of sarcasm. It sounds funny now, but as a ten-year-old girl, this hurt a lot. The takeaway is that I always remember being bullied as a young girl and always try to make the acquaintance of, and be an advocate for, a student who I observe placed in that weaker social position at school. I go out of my way to make sure that other students see that student is cared about, accepted, respected, and feels important in my class.

Parents have a responsibility to raise kind kids. Kids start ripping each other apart in school from very young. Identifying the weaker kids and trying to raise them up in school, giving them a group or a club that they can fit into, can be a huge game changer for students on the fringes. Knowing they have a voice somewhere in the school community can be that tether of hope that will help them to sleep at night.

There was a time when Dana and I were very unkind to a boy in our class. He had the highest grades and a very involved mother, relative to what was common parental input in the 1970s. Because of this, he took a lot of abuse. Even Dana and I took the opportunity to bully this boy, to make ourselves feel we were higher up on the social ladder in some way. We made angel wings out of hangers and tin foil and ran after him one day attempting to hook them onto his jacket. It was mean-spirited of us, and we did get in trouble. I know I did it to feel like I had some type of power in that classroom over someone. It was wrong, and I know we both have always regretted our actions that day.

As a society, we need to do better, be kinder, more gentle. Not everyone has the grit that I was able to dig up and maintain to survive. This is exactly why we have so many children committing suicide. On top of what was happening at school, I also felt that I couldn't lean on my mom because of her own life experiences. One time early on, I came home crying and told my mom what had been happening to me. She became visibly upset, and that made me feel like I needed to spare my mom from the reality of my school life, because she had enough of her own problems to deal with. Even at that young age, I understood that my mom was emotionally fragile at times, and I didn't want to upset her. I didn't understand all the circumstances surrounding my experiences as a child. My mom's loss of her family, her sadness or depression because of that loss, a time when bullies were accepted as a rite of passage, and standing up to them on your own was a part of being a successful kid. There was nowhere to go for shelter.

One night I was crying in bed, praying to God to take me and to just let me die, so I could go to Heaven and be with Jesus. As I was praying and crying, an angel appeared in my bedroom closet; the one sliding wood door had been open. The angel was iridescent white and had wings visible on her back. She was definitely female and was facing sideways so that I could see her profile and wings. When I was young, I believed it was the Blessed Mother. But after a lifetime of my mother's vignettes that enabled me to know my Grandma Dorothy, I believe it was her. No words were spoken, but there was telepathic communication between this angel and myself. "Everything will be alright. I am with you and watching over you always." I remember this like it was yesterday. I immediately felt like a weight had been lifted off my chest, and I felt like I had a way to go on, knowing someone was with me and protecting me. I knew then that I wasn't all alone. My sister, Dena, witnessed this event. Years later, Dena confirmed that she remembered seeing the same angel in our closet that night, but she didn't receive any "message," as I did.

That was the first of several times my life was touched by divine intervention or unexplainable events. The common thread between each is that, in the moment, I couldn't see my way forward and felt truly lost and hopeless.

Kids need to see their parents sacrifice for them. This is what really gives a child a feeling of self-worth. When a child sees a parent go without money or time to be there for them, this is what really creates the bond between children and their parents and gives them the true feeling within themselves that they are worth something and are worthy of love. In my opinion, when children don't experience this, low self-esteem will develop. They won't develop the feeling that they deserve happiness or are worthy of possessing the things they desire. These children are the children who will have more difficulty in school and will get involved in negative relationships.

Over the years, I have taught many students who immigrated from other countries. These students saw the sacrifices their parents made to make sure they would have a better life and it helped these kids believe in themselves and work hard in school. Even parents who struggle with money can show their children they are important to them – by spending time with them or by going without things for themselves to make sure their child has a fresh pair of sneakers or a new coat. These children gain a sense of security and self-worth, knowing that they are important to their parents and thus, worthy of love.

It is important that a child feels important to their parents and sees this in their actions. Sharing time and resources with them shows that.

Almost all parents love their children, but some have trouble sharing. Children with parents who love them, but are living in an adult-centered home where the wants and needs of the parents always come first, may feel undeserving. This forms a negative narrative in their minds. In contrast, parents who give their children everything because they have the resources, but do not give them their time, regularly suffer from low expectations in relationships. This influences the child's goals in life and what they believe they can achieve.

Parents who don't sacrifice their time to spend with their children also create children with low self-worth. Another group is parents who break promises, regularly letting down their kids by not showing up or not coming through. This type of parent damages their child's ability to build healthy relationships. This happened to my son, Alex, over and over. He would wait by the window for his dad to show up at the promised time and would be let down more times than I can remember. The sad face and body language walking away from the window when he finally gave up hoping he would come, would break my heart.

Low self-esteem and negative self-efficacy develop in adult-centered homes. When kids see their parents' hobbies and interests indulged, but theirs are not, a covert message is being sent about their importance. This influences their beliefs about how they see themselves in the future.

There were times when a book from the Scholastic book order could have done a lot for my self-esteem. Sitting in class when your classmates are receiving their new books, and your parents didn't think a new book was necessary, is hurtful and embarrassing. It's a chance to RAISE your child that has been missed. These small things help cement the feeling of unworthiness that we need to be aware of in children. Children need to see people sacrifice in small ways for them, such as buying them a book through school, and it also sends a message that reading and education are important. Be kind and cognizant of the messages you are giving the young people who see you through your actions.

What does sacrifice have to do with being kind? When you are kind, you are sharing something of yourself with another person. It may be your time, resources, energy, or emotions. It's whatever that person at that moment may need, and it's up to you to recognize what you can do to help if you want to make a difference.

When I was about ten years old, I started working on Saturdays for a woman who lived down the block from us. Amelia was a kind lady and could see that I needed *something*. She offered me a job cleaning her building's hallways and also dusting and cleaning the furniture in her apartment. I would save my money and buy things I wanted to have with the money she paid me. She also had a hot dog truck and would give me snacks and Sabrett hot dogs now and then. She was kind to me and gave me an opportunity to develop my self-worth, self-esteem, and my self-efficacy, and helped me to develop, early on, a work ethic that has served me well in life and also influenced my character – which may have saved my life.

From early on, I always felt that I had to take care of myself and find a way to earn what I wanted on my own. A large chip developed on my shoulder, and I had an attitude that I didn't need or want anyone to help me. I've always been prideful, and if I had to ask more than once for something, I wouldn't be able to accept it with the same feeling if I felt I had to push for it. However, that was just the hard shell covering up the excessive softness inside. This understanding has served me well in my profession as a teacher. The harder the shell, the softer the filling. These were some of the first life lessons that helped me develop the empathy I would need to understand the children that would be in front of me in the far-off years ahead. The chip started because deep down, I felt that my parents, particularly my father, didn't want to share his resources. Simply put, he was a bit selfish. My mom loved him with all her heart, but I think she recognized this as well at times. My parents were deeply in love with each other for sure. They would kiss in the mornings by the kitchen sink. They really had deep passion in their marriage, which put a lot of pressure on my expectation of what a marriage should be. Mom did sacrifice for us and would sneak packages into the house with items that my dad would not approve of. After he passed, my mom spent a lot of money and shared much of what she was left with all of us. She said she wanted us to enjoy our inheritance and not wait until she was gone. When I look back in reflection as an adult, my dad also sacrificed for me, but not in ways that a child would understand. I was also the starter child, the oldest, and my parents did change their stance with my sisters. My sister, Noel, pointed out to me that my parents didn't have peers with children the same age as I was, so there was no barometer for what would be deemed average for a child in the 70-80's to reasonably need to fit in socially. When my younger sister was growing up, one of Dad's best friends, Ray, had children the same age, and that seemed to help him gauge what was average or appropriate for the time. The small things, like the book from the school fair or a pair of shoes, would please the wearer, not the purchaser. This was something that I was honestly cognizant of, and my low self-esteem stemmed from it. My feelings and opinions were not recognized as important.

When it was time to graduate high school, I wanted to go to a trade school, not necessarily college, at that time. I wanted to go to Katharine Gibbs, which was a school for secretarial work; today's terminology is an administrative assistant. With an associate degree from Katherine Gibbs, my job opportunities would have been much more lucrative than just graduating from high school with typing and steno as my skill set. My dad and I went and checked out the program. On the car ride home, he told me that it was too expensive to send me there. I already had that chip on my shoulder because I felt that I had to do things for myself. My pride and inability to accept help were becoming a barrier for me at this point. Feeling like someone was giving me something begrudgingly was a major issue for me. I wouldn't ask twice for anything. If the immediate response wasn't the message, "Sure, we can do that," or "Don't worry, we'll get it done," I wanted no part. This moment in the car really synthesized that. I vividly remember just feeling so low, and my heart actually hurt, knowing that my father wouldn't sacrifice his resources to send me to this school. That was a crushing blow for me at the time. I held it in, and my parents didn't know how hurt I was because I had already built my wall, more like a rampart, to hide my true emotions. It was another notch in the belt of, "This is my life, and I'm going to do it for myself. I'm not going to ask anyone for help anymore."

I've always wondered why my dad didn't say, "We can get a student loan, and when you are done, you can pay it back." It's hard for me to understand why he didn't just say that to me that day. I wish he was alive for me to ask him what he was thinking. He was a college graduate; he had to know there were other options and ways to pay for this school which would have given me a leg up and a better chance at a career. It's one of those things I'll never really understand. It may have been life-changing for me. I would have been living at home and going to school for two more years.

There was another very critical time when I asked my parents for help. I was going through a custody battle with my ex, and I needed a lawyer. My parents couldn't help me at the time and told me that my son would be better off splitting time between the two families. Ultimately, I lost daily custody of Alex for a period of time, as earlier mentioned, and only had him on weekends. That was another very traumatic time in life for both Alex and myself. The repercussions of that period of time in my life were monumental. However, I now know that it was part of what my life was to be – to gain those experiences by going through many trials and tribulations with Alex through his youth and teen years. All these experiences are now part of my war chest. I have to believe it was purely a predetermined destiny at work to make my message today possible.

After graduating high school at seventeen, I started working at Morgan Guarantee as a money transfer editor, checking the numbers on wire transfers all day long. It was a very boring job. After work, I would hop on the PATH train and walk the few blocks from Journal Square to Alex's house. His mother and father were like parents to me while Alex and I were a couple. Once I crossed over to an adversary, not so much. They were loyal to their son, and I have to respect that. The only thing I will fault them with is their role in taking my son away from me. That was wrong, but I know it was emotional, and they had their side as well.

For the time I was part of their family, Alex's parents treated me like a daughter. After my son Alex arrived, my father-in-law would pick me up from Rutgers in Newark when I started taking classes. He told me he wouldn't let me take the PATH train home at night from Newark. It's actually funny that he was worried about me, because I can't even recall where my ex was back then. He should have been the one picking me up. My father-in-law would call me "Miss America." He was quiet, introspective, hard-working, and kind. Helen, my mother-in-law, was a devoted mother who would go to the outer ends of the earth for her children – to a fault. She spoiled them all, including her grandson, my son Alex.

When Alex and I split up, we were all fighting over my son Alex. I believe we were all trying to do what we thought was best for him at the time, but the person who suffered most was Alex. His paternal grandparents have both passed away now. Going back thirty-five years and being a grandparent now myself, I understand they loved him and wanted to make sure that he was in their lives. Both my father-in-law and mother-in-law, Papou and Yaya, were very good people and parents that didn't give up on their children – no matter what. What they didn't consider was the importance of a small child being with their mother, and that damaging that mother-son bond will really hurt a child psychologically. I know they didn't think of that at the time; they were just trying to keep "their family" together.

Yaya was a dedicated and hardworking mother. She told me about how she met Papou at church. She was eighteen and living with her stepmother and father, who had sponsored her to come to the US from Greece. He and his second wife were treating her like an indentured servant. After meeting Papou at church, during their one and only meet up over coffee, Papou proposed marriage, and she accepted.

She told me they met at the courthouse the next day, and right before they went in to apply for the marriage license, Papou asked if she was a virgin. When she said, "Yes," he said, "Then come with me." She would joke and say, "I should have turned around and left when he asked me that." Years after the dust had cleared, Papou and Yaya bought Anthony and I a washer and dryer as a housewarming present. They also once lent us money when we were behind on our mortgage in the early years. I give them credit on both ends of the spectrum as far as being supportive. They helped us because they were ensuring things would be stable for their grandson.

There was a time when I was really hurt by Yaya's actions, but I also understand when I look at it through the lens of a mother acting on behalf of her children. I understand why she did the things she did. She was a mother first. No matter what one of her children or grandchildren did, right or wrong, she backed up her offspring like a mother bear guarding her cubs.

Once she had her own family, she made sure the things that really hurt her and damaged her were not done to her own children. This was something I definitely took from her playbook and followed. She ended up overcompensating to make sure the things that hurt her were not felt by her own children. I am guilty of that, too, at times.

She was a powerhouse who would work all day in the fashion district in New York as a furrier, sewing fur coats, come home and cook dinner for her boys, and also do seamstress work from home. I admired her tenacity regarding her boys. At the end of her life, we came back together and made peace with each other. I know she watches over my son, his wife, and my grandchildren, and that's enough for me.

I've taken a piece from the playbooks of various women I met throughout my life. From my mother-in-law Helen, it was how to protect my young – to do my best to make sure the things that really stood out as damaging to my development, would not happen to my own children. My success has come through supporting and encouraging all my children to get an education. However I could, to the best of my ability, I have tried to make that a reality for each of them – be it through revising essays for scholarships, filling out FAFSA forms, researching colleges, talking endlessly about programs and possible paths, and never giving up on their education, dreams, or goals. For my three children, this has been a primary focus. It has been a keen focus of mine to be sure each one of them knew that I would help pay for their education, whatever type they wanted. Both Alex and Gia moved through college and master's degrees without too many twists and turns. Gia is currently researching Ph.D. programs to continue *their education and become a psychologist.

My middle child Jake has had a more tumultuous relationship with academia. After attending Montclair University as a freshman, then transferring to New Jersey City University for the first semester of sophomore year, he withdrew toward the end of that semester wasting his time and our money. He later attended Rutgers Coding Bootcamp and earned a Commercial Driver's License. We figured he needed some time to figure out what he really wanted to do. He is currently completing an IT degree at New Jersey Institute of Technology. We've always known that Jake wants to sell his game ideas and be a game designer. Finding a game design program is really a tall order in this part of the country. Jake has been working on a tabletop game for years and has started a game company with his friend Sean. Eventually, they will get their games into production and available for sale. Jake has always shared his game ideas with me over the years – they recently had a prototype made for the most recent game he and Sean invented. Jake asked me to play it with him to try it out. It was fun and fast moving. He's an artist and an inventor and is going to school to get a paying job in IT that will enable him to invest in his game ideas and get them into production. He thinks outside the box and wants to create something of his own. Jake and Sean are an impressive team. They already have prototypes of two games and many more they can pull the trigger on quickly.

The bottom line is all three of my children were supported in their educational endeavors and goals for what they wanted to do with their lives to the best of our ability. I never wanted any of them to feel the way I felt when my dad told me he couldn't afford to send me to Katharine Gibbs. We all take from our backstories. I never got a chance to talk with my dad about this, and I imagine he had something in his backstory that made him worried about taking out student loans. He must have had a reason to justify his decision.

In addition to looking out for my own children, I carry all my experiences into my classroom to use organically, as a teachable moment, or sometimes formally included in my lesson plans. Each day I try to pull from my past and model for the younger people in front of me so that they can move up and out of their current situation and into a life they can imagine for themselves. It's important that they know someone in their life that has accomplished this. That's why I use my backstory in my classroom. I share moments and times in my life of how I changed my narrative from a student on the margins to a successful professional as a real-world example of what is possible.

There were many women who influenced me, including my devoted, stay-at-home mother who loved us all very much. As I grew and matured, I've learned to better understand my mother and the things that drove her, such as her own early life. She lost her parents, a sibling, and her grandfather in the span of three years, by the age of nineteen. My mother would go into a frenzy now and then, which scared me and caused me to conceal my outward emotions. At the time, I didn't see the light at the end of the tunnel. But my mom's difficult life and sad experiences, through fate, turned me into the person I was supposed to be. Because of my mother, I've been able to tap into this empathy and help so many children.

Dealing with intense tears, highly emotional moments, and stressful situations, I developed an automatic pilot mode. In retrospect, this is what has made me a very effective teacher of students with behavior and emotional disorders. These types of classes can be very chaotic, erratic, and emotionally charged – they can change from calm to total chaos with the brush of a hand taken the wrong way. These upsetting times are difficult for me to process, so I go into automatic pilot mode and do not engage emotionally in the situation. While I somehow remain present for safety, I am able to disengage my emotions and stay clinical while chaos ensues around me. This coping mechanism I developed as a young child has served me well in my professional career as a special education teacher, but it has hurt me as a mother at times. When delivering very bad news, I may laugh. I don't mean to laugh, it is simply a coping mechanism I've developed. My children, at times, have perceived me as disengaged or reacting inappropriately during times of high emotion within our family dynamic. My coping mechanism stops me from feeling in the moment. I feel extreme, deep emotions later, after the dust settles. I will cry alone at night, but it takes me some time to process the things that are happening around me.

Sometimes I cry when I shouldn't. I could be in the middle of telling a story to friends, when something I've been trying to process for years suddenly becomes blatantly clear. Cue the tears. I am no psychologist, but I know this goes back to my early childhood and feeling I had to keep it together for my mother.

When there is chaos and erratic behavior around me, I shut off emotionally and go on autopilot. My emotions are processed at a later time when no one is watching. This leaves some people observing what appears to be a detached person, which I am not. I may be delayed, but I am not detached.

I have recognized a similarity in some of my students through the years – how they react, or specifically don't react, when the class goes into one of these tailspins. I easily identify those students who appear to have a similar backstory to mine, and I will pull from that knowledge to talk with them, and hopefully, reach them.

"Now gently settles like dust in a shaft – for one moment, there is no one else – only the wind like the hiss on an ice skate…" John Geddes

At that moment of chaos, there is a look in someone's eyes that I recognize as if we are both traveling back in time to where it all began for each of us – when it felt as if a lightning bolt struck and ended their childhood. Two people locked in an unspoken understanding. I sear it in my mind and return to that student later when the chaos is over. Then I begin trying to unlock what is holding them back from their true potential, from feeling their rightful self-esteem, or from developing a positive image of themselves for the future.

You can't learn empathy from a college textbook. It's cultivated by your life's experiences. There is no blame for anyone. Every single person in your backstory, my backstory, has helped us become who we are today. Whether the experience was positive or negative, you took something from it. If I didn't experience chaotic, emotionally-stifling episodes, I wouldn't be able to recognize those emotions in students, and be able to connect with them through the years. I know my students felt that I really understood and cared about them because I could reach back in my mind, put myself in their shoes, walk their walk, and talk their talk.

I consider each of my life experiences a blessing because I've put them to use in my classroom for over twenty years now. My understanding of the Universe tells me that Candace's mom, Janet, who was a teacher, is not offended by my recollections, but is satisfied knowing that her influence on me has changed lives for the better. All the parts of my backstory have come together to put the wheels in motion, helping me mentor students who are trying to stretch by allowing them to feel accepted, cared about, and comfortable to share their secrets with me at times and helping them take the initial risk to move up and out of being sequestered.

In a self-contained classroom, my students and I grow very close because we spend the majority of the day together, often including lunch. In a packet I received at a Jersey City Board of Education Special Education Department workshop, I learned about a powerful talking and sharing technique that I have facilitated in my self-contained classrooms ever since.

Speaker Power begins with everyone sitting in a circle. A student is chosen to hold a soft pillow which gives them the floor to share whatever they want to talk about – whether something that happened at dinner last night or their brother's problems.

Everyone in the room promises that what is said in the room will stay in the room. I explain that if I feel anyone is in danger or going to harm themselves, I will have to follow up outside of the room. All participants must agree before we begin. No one is permitted to comment or add to what the "Speaker" shares unless the "Speaker" invites them to do so. That is the "Power."

If comments or questions were not wanted, the "Speaker" would pass the pillow to the next student. If they were willing to talk, they would hold the pillow. If they didn't want to share, they would pass it. And so it went. As the facilitator, I started off by holding the pillow and sharing about what was going on in my life. This was many years ago now, and at that time, there was plenty of material in my own home to share with my cayenne pepper son, Alex, and his teenage antics. I would openly share my troubles and how upset and scared I was at times, including my emotions and feelings as a parent when it came to Alex's escapades.. I would always hold the pillow and take questions from my class. Only after their last question had been answered, would I pass the pillow. Most of the time, I would answer every question. If it became too personal, I would say, "too personal," but that was very rare. I have always treated my life as an open book, as you may surmise.

This sharing time was so powerful in one particular class. I'll always remember how much this time of the day helped my students. As expected, it started off slow with only one or two sharing a little at first. But as the days and weeks went on, we kept at it. Little by little, the students began sharing very deep and private traumatic events in their lives and releasing the hurt and trauma into the group. Most times, questions were not taken and the pillow was passed. But each student held the power of simply releasing, being heard, and being acknowledged and validated – with a hug, a nod, or maybe a tissue being handed to them or used by someone else in the circle. This opportunity for sharing and truly being heard is a powerful strategy in enabling my students to move on from being locked in emotionally stifling memories.

My first Speaker Power was a long time ago, and I haven't always had classes where I could use this sharing circle. But when my classes included students who I suspected were struggling with past trauma and/or with emotional and behavioral issues, this technique added real value for my students. As the facilitator, I was able to openly and honestly share my story, display true empathy, and effectively set the lead for my students to follow – using my backstory to pay it forward.

It's not easy to break open the hard shells of children who have erected very high walls or even ramparts after being so damaged by trauma. Some will never break. Yet, others will, maybe after weeks or even months of helping to lay the groundwork, will begin to open, and you will see a rose bloom right before your eyes.

Kids develop very thick shells to protect themselves from the past hurts and let downs they have experienced. The first class that took the Speaker Power journey with me all those years ago was an amazing group of children. They are a group of warriors for wellness, and the work we did together was truly life-changing for me and, I believe, for them as well. I can't say their names here, but I will always remember each and every one of them.

Through the years, I've had the opportunity to use the Speaker Power sharing circle with success. When it's implemented with fidelity, and there is true sharing and listening, a bond quickly builds between the participants. The students seem calmer all day after being given time to get baggage they were holding from the past, or even the night before, off their chests. And this positivity traveled with the students throughout the school day. Stronger relationships among the students developed, and the children looked out for each other as if they were truly a family. I would use this technique coupled with making small treats. Using small kitchen appliances such as a waffle maker or an electric stove top burner, I made the students pizza, grilled cheese sandwiches, and quesadilla-type items. These small meals, combined with Speaker Power conducted first thing in the morning, laid the groundwork for classrooms that resembled families. I am proud of those days and the work I did in classrooms through the years. I hope that talking about my experiences will inspire other teachers who are interested in tapping into their own backstories to fuel the talk to help their students heal. While general education teachers can make use of some of these ideas as well, note that these ideas and strategies work best within small classes with eight to ten students at most.

There are many other lessons I learned through my own deviant behaviors that have changed the way I respond in situations. Things that can make my fellow teachers crazy, I can let roll off my back – chalking it up to "they needed it more than me" – and keep going. I give the situation a small bit of energy, reflect for a moment on my past life, then let it all go.

Students will sometimes steal items from their teachers. They are young, and some kids don't have the things they think they deserve and need, like, a phone charger, a pack of gum, money, food, whatever it may be. When these instances happen, I don't allow myself to be upset. I think back to the days when I would take things that I shouldn't have taken because I felt at that moment I needed it. Coins from a jar from kids I was babysitting, socks from McCrory's, fifty dollars twice from my high school job, quarters from my dad's desk. I've taken things that I shouldn't have, and I've returned what I could years later when I realized it was wrong.

The point is, when I took those things, I thought I *really needed* them. I wasn't a bad kid, just in a situation that made me think it's what I had to do to get what I thought I needed at the moment. I own that. Yet, I continue to tap into all of my past shared experiences when I know one of my students has taken something from me.

A colleague once stole an idea of mine – a strategy I devised to help students write a narrative essay over the course of an entire month. I used it with a class of students that needed to see that they could do it, but could only handle one sentence a day. We did it, and they had an entire essay written after a month. A fellow teacher at my school put the concept into her portfolio as if it were her own. When I confronted her, she gaslighted me – even though the outline for the essay was in my own handwriting *in her portfolio.* Yet again, when managing those feelings of anger, I say to myself, "I guess they needed it more than I did."

Chapter 13: The Crossroad

I went to visit Michelle after she had her first baby. I had been a bridesmaid in her wedding party and considered her to be one of my very best friends at the time. When I arrived, Michelle and her husband, Charlie, were behaving very out of character. They didn't hug or kiss me on the cheek as usual, and when I asked to hold her newborn baby, she refused. I knew it was because of the HIV scare and I remember at that moment feeling rejected and humiliated.

It is a horrible feeling for someone to not want to touch you because they are frightened they could catch a deadly disease. That rejection and humiliation are still felt today when I reflect on that visit. However, that was a big moment and a big lesson for me to learn but it didn't end our friendship. I now knew that people were looking at me differently, and now I was treated differently. It hurt.

Again, I look at that negative interaction and, in my memory, made it a positive experience because it taught a valuable lesson about humility and compassion when dealing with people that have diseases and/or illnesses, psychological disorders, physical handicaps, cognitive impairments, and learning disabilities and any of the other plethora of issues that come up in a teacher's life. Treat each person with care and never make someone feel rejected or humiliated because of an illness, tick, or condition that they have. Give each person you come into contact with eye contact and the kindness of a personal greeting that will put them at ease.

When reflecting on development and the id, ego, and superego. A few things went wrong that shaped how I saw myself and my place in the world. Three critical requests shaped my negative self-efficacy. The shoes, school book orders, and my education. These became three pillars for me going forward, and those who really know what makes me tick, such as my kids and my sisters, know this.

I was never a person too involved or interested in designer labels. I'll buy a shirt at Walmart and wear a Longchamp purse with it. However, I've always had a thing for shoes, and the shoes that I put on my offspring's feet must be stylish and of quality. I detest cheap shoes. Where does that come from? Perhaps the event outside of Hyman's Shoe Store when I threw myself in the gutter because my mother wanted me to have sturdy lace-up baby walkers when I was three? Then there is the issue of books. Being overindulgent regarding children's books for my own children and the amount of books that I've bought for my classroom through the years is well into the thousands. When the load gets too much for my small house, I make baskets and put them outside my house with a note saying "Free." I really don't think I have ever said "No" in response to a request for a book from anyone. The last is education; all three of my kids were told from very young that they were going to college or whatever program they wanted to pursue, no matter what, we'd find a way to pay for it, and I've kept my promises to the best of my ability.

Somehow these moments in my life when I was told "NO" had a huge impact on me. Why? I really can't say, but they have, so I've classically overcompensated with my own children to make sure these are not the things they remember me by. Of course, in my zest to make sure I wouldn't make the same mistakes my parents made, I've made plenty of my own along the way. Gia has recently shared with me they were made fun of at school for having too many books and items in their book orders. The irony shocked me and my mouth dropped open.

Being a parent is a slippery slope, and it's not easy to know what to do each time there is a decision to be made. Thinking about what is important to me, I think that my ego is pretty pragmatic. Anthony will keep me up to date with what is going on with celebrities, musicians, and basically anything to do with pop culture. My reality and what I am concerned with is very functional. If it isn't something I can use regularly, then I most likely don't want it; a minimalist to my core. Engaging in worry about things that I have no control over and nonsense don't interest me in the least. Drama and gossip literally exhaust me.

There was a time in my life when I was very religious. Worrying about going to church to have attendance taken each week was a true consideration of mine. I don't know how that developed, but it did. Always wanting to belong to something may have played a part. For a time, I became very involved in fundraising and event planning for a local Catholic parish, and also taught Sunday school classes. It may have developed because there was a time when my church as well turned its back on me. Going to confession when you are a Roman Catholic is a way to rid yourself of guilt, and it is rare when a priest will not absolve you of your sins.

About twenty-four years ago, I went to confession, and the priest would not absolve me of my sins. I promise you I have not committed murder. It was because I didn't have my first marriage, which was in a Greek Orthodox Church, annulled before I married Anthony. This was a high point in hypocrisy to me. The Roman Catholic Church would not marry Alex and me because he was not Catholic. He would have had to convert, and that wasn't going to happen. The Greek Orthodox Church agreed to marry us without asking me to convert from my religion, so that's what we did. Years pass, and we are divorced. I'm married to Anthony civilly, and our wedding ceremony was conducted by a retired Catholic priest. That was enough for both of us to feel that our marriage was sealed by GOD. When I went to confession, I was told that I was going to burn in Hell forever, so I left there crying and started the process of getting an annulment from the Roman Catholic Church. After the money was paid and several intense interviews, asking very personal questions of the witnesses I had to supply to attest to and recount relevant events, the marriage was annulled.

Anthony and I were then married, for the second time, in the Roman Catholic Church quietly and had a small reception at George's Pub and Grub on a weekday evening with only our immediate families there. All this was done at the urging of my son, Alex. He was going to Mt. Carmel Catholic School at the time and was worried about the turn of the millennium and wanted all of our souls to be in line with the Church at the time, including his own. There was a time when he wore a scapula every day and wanted to convert to Roman Catholic from Greek Orthodox as well. Again, a very big superego coupled with a soft heart encased in a hard shell for protection. All this is a consequence of being hurt and let down, hiding underneath the cayenne pepper "spicy" behavior. All because of the parental fighting over custody that unnecessarily hurt his ego and superego enormously.

As you can see, digression is real. We were all put neatly in order with the Church in response to Alex's pleas. My mom had been teaching Sunday school and was getting ready to retire from the position and asked me if I'd like to take over, and I did. Teaching Sunday school led me to the Church community and the community events for the children, such as the Halloween party to start. This was how I became friendly with the pastor of the church at the time. I would talk honestly about my life and the issues and problems I was having. This priest gave me books and introduced me to contemplation. I was always able to pray and meditate, but this was something deeper. We had sessions where

169

he would coach me through contemplation and times when we would contemplate together.

Over time he became too involved in my life and was demanding a lot of my time. We would spend a lot of time together contemplating, talking, driving around, and going to bookstores to buy books on the topic, visiting historical parks and museums. On my own time, I was contemplating for several hours on some days and was becoming very submerged in practice, believing I was getting very good at it. I was able to close my eyes and focus on GOD, and my soul would travel upward. I would sense my spirit leaving my body, and my mind would become immersed in a total connection with GOD. There were no spoken words but a deep feeling of peace and safety. There were times when I felt as if I had gone through many levels and was getting closer to understanding GOD's true essence. The priest would ask me to contemplate with him, hold his hands, and go into a meditative state together. A few of the books he gave me included "The Cloud of Unknowing," a book about St. John of the Cross and Saint Teresa of Avila and the relationship they shared together. They had a marriage of prayer in a sense. In many ways, he did educate me on contemplation and the seven castles that must be passed through to come to total enlightenment with GOD. I've read about thirty books on the subject, most of which I have given away. The only books I kept are the "Cloud of Unknowing," and a few books about particular saints and the Gnostic Gospels. If you are truly interested in contemplation, I suggest you read this book which is a book about Christian mysticism; the author is unknown.

As my teacher, he would explain how we were having a relationship similar to these two saints. They loved each other through their prayer and contemplative connection. Obviously, this was ridiculous. I am no saint, and neither was he. However, at the time, he was my spiritual advisor and priest, and I had put all my faith into him and what he was teaching me about mysticism, contemplation, and Kabbalah. Each religion has its own version of the same thing, which has a goal of complete union with GOD.

Around 2007, I had a near-death experience. I had traveled and was literally in the arms of Jesus and was given a choice to continue living with my family or to stay with Jesus, at that moment for all eternity. I decided to stay with my family because my children were all still too young for me to voluntarily leave them, and immediately, my spirit was returned to my body which was lying in my bed. However, the decision was given to me. I was literally being cradled in the arms of Jesus. The sense of peace and tranquility and the feeling of total wholeness truly filled me with a level of awe that evades me to describe. There were no spoken words but a sense of telepathy as communication. Thoughts were read. This was the type of traveling that was going on with no drugs involved. I returned to my family and continued to contemplate for hours at a time. One night soon thereafter, I was contemplating, and the room filled with heavy black smoke. I knew that an evil entity had entered my room and that I had turned into a place where I should not be. Immediately calling out, "JESUS, SAVE ME!" and in that second, the smoke disappeared. At that moment, I said, "No more." I'll meditate, but no contemplation anymore. The books warn that if you are not truly ready, or lack the knowledge and discipline, you can get into trouble, just as I did. It is a wonderful thing to know it's true and to have had an experience like this. I have no doubt that GOD exists, that Heaven and the afterlife are real, and I am not at all scared to die. I want to stay with my family as long as possible, but I am not scared to go because I know for sure that GOD exists.

Another sign that my family is on the other side of this world, watching and waiting, happened when I was having an argument with Anthony. Our marriage was in serious trouble because of Father Gerry. He had been swaying me away from my marriage when I had originally gone to him for help in strengthening my marriage. I was about to tell Anthony that Father Gerry and I were going to contemplate off into the sunset, like Saint Teresa of Avila and St. John of the Cross. Just as I was about to tell Anthony, someone or something – unseen to both of us – swatted my eye and literally cut my eyeball to the point that I had to go to the emergency room. This ended the argument on the spot, before I could utter my next sentence that was on deck in my mind. At the hospital, I was told that my eye was cut and I had to wear an eyepatch. That was a moment when I was about to end my marriage because I was confused and mixed up about what was happening in my prayer life with Father Gerry. As my "spiritual advisor," he was leading me to believe that my contemplative life was a calling from GOD, and I was considering devoting my life to its practice. I definitely was developing a deeper relationship with GOD, but this priest was trying to lead me down the wrong path away from my family. I needed to be removed from this relationship with him to look back and be able to see things more clearly.

Chapter 14: More Lessons to Learn

After passing through an extremely religious period in my life, I turned to a more spiritual and less dogmatic way of thinking about God. During the year or so, as I was developing my meditation and contemplative skills, Alex and his girlfriend, Laura, were starting off in college. Laura was living with us for about a year because her mother had passed away and her aunt had taken the money meant for Laura. Her aunt would see me around town and make the sign of the cross like she was a saint and I was some type of heretic. I had looked out for Laura, made sure she started college, and made sure she was OK at the time. I loved Laura as if she was one of my own. Alex and Laura would fight and bring chaos into the household, which was really inappropriate for Jake and Gia to be subjected to at this point. Anthony and I decided it was time to try a dose of tough love. So we rented a U-haul truck and packed up Alex's room, and sent him to go live with his Yaya for a time. He was really stretching his wings at this time, and even Yaya couldn't handle him. She made him leave her house as well. Laura had gone to live with her aunt at this point, and Alex and his friends, Kyle and Brian, rented an apartment together. At the time, my ex was remarried to LoriAnn, who worked for the Division of Youth and Family Services (DYFS), and she filed a complaint against us for putting Alex out at the time. LoriAnn was clearly seeking revenge. She and my ex both knew about Alex's all-night shenanigans and that it was inappropriate for our younger children to witness. A DYFS worker was sent out to investigate our family. This was very hurtful, considering she knew how much I loved Alex and what I had gone through years earlier to fight for custody of him. We had to make the hard choice of practicing tough love with Alex. We could not risk DYFS taking our younger, impressionable children away because of Alex's antics. We had to be responsible parents for all involved.

The DYFS worker showed up out of the blue one night when we were having pizza for my mother's birthday. They interviewed both Jake and Gia privately and looked through our house, in our refrigerator, cabinets, and bedrooms. After they left, Gia and Jake told us they were asked if they were fed properly. They both responded, "Look at us. Do we look like our parents aren't feeding us?" They were also asked about how we treated them, Alex and Laura's relationship, and my relationship with the priest. The kids told them what they could through the lens of eight and ten-year-old kids.

The point is that this was another one of those terrible moments that taught me a huge life lesson that I would use going forward as a teacher. That lesson is to proceed with extreme care when calling or thinking about calling Child Services. Separating children from their parents should not be taken lightly. All families go through issues at one time or another. The more perfect a family seems often correlates with more underlying problems that are lurking unseen. As a teacher, it is important to talk with parents and see if there is anything they may need help with, give them phone numbers of places to get assistance, and be willing to support them by getting them information that can help them.

Being on the other side of that call made me cognizant of thinking about the other side of this story, and what could possibly be started when making that call. That was eye-opening for me and will forever remain an act of revenge that was really unforgivable. My ex's wife was not the mother of any of the children concerned and made that call out of revenge because my son was going to be a pain in her ass and upend her life at the time, because he may have had to go live with his father and her for a time. Alex, at nineteen, needed a dose of tough love at that point in his life, and my younger children needed to be kept safe. Unfortunately, Alex Sr.'s second wife passed away. I was never able to clear the air with her or able to forgive her for that move. However, she did help other children going forward by teaching me a tough lesson. Never leave a student in harm's way, but understanding the ebb and flow of real blended family life, with its ups and downs, and how a parent feels when faced with a DYFS situation, has been helpful. Being able to empathize has helped pave the way to have honest talks with parents about what they can or want to do because of the unique situation they find themselves in. To bring things back around. Being extremely lucky, GOD stepped in and spared me from a life of addiction. I haven't always been the perfect mother, but that didn't mean my child would have been better off in foster care at that time. I needed a little time to pull myself together. Remembering those moments makes my chest swell as I write this. Having been there is a huge blessing that has helped me never forget how far I've come.

Sometimes giving parents a little support – the phone number of an agency that can help with the cost of college or trade school, information about an after-school program that can cover their gap in childcare, or just listening to get a handle on what the real issue is so that you can assist them to problem solve – is all they need to curtail a situation from becoming a bigger problem. I've had children tell me terrible stories about things that have happened to them in foster care over the years and how much they would have rather been able to stay with their own parents, problems and all.

Chapter 15: Learning Unconditional Acceptance

Learning to accept Gia's alternative life choices has been a journey for the whole family. Jake has always been most supportive of Gia and has let me know when I haven't been as supportive or accepting as I thought I was. When Gia told me they were in a relationship with a girl for several years, with someone I thought was a platonic friend, I was a little disappointed but quickly accepted the reality. Anthony and I were accepting of their relationship and found a silver lining in the fact that we didn't have to worry about teen pregnancy. We thought it was a phase that would most likely pass. As time went on, I believe Gia was bringing us along slowly. The next level of awareness came when Gia put a poster on their bedroom door announcing that they were pansexual, and there were explanations on the notice about how they felt held back by the family and wanted to be accepted for who they were. This all came as a shock to me, and I found the terminology confusing, but we tried our best to explain to Gia that we love them and all we really want is for them to be a good person and to do good things in this world. To live a good life and make some type of positive difference. To be happy, independent, self-sufficient, and find love. We really mean that for all our kids. As they were growing up, I left family parties rather than fight over my liberal views with relatives about interracial marriage, being open to the idea and acknowledging that all religions have truth and should be honored equally, understanding that we all believe in the same one GOD but depending on where our families came from changes the narrative we follow, and being accepting of fluid labels to express who you are and how you identify. I've come to understand that there is no talking to certain people. My absence from a conversation – that is really just bashing and not a conversation at all – and removing myself from the situation, says more about me than engaging with people who just want to tell you why you are wrong.

Gia is a transgender man, and his name is Ben in life outside our home. Gia had helped me to understand a lot about how he came to this realization – including how, as a young child, they never felt comfortable being called "she" and being treated differently than their brothers. As a small child and young teen Gia was "a girly girl," in my opinion. Gia explained to me that they were hyper-assimilating to their gender assignment at birth to go along and cover up their true feelings. There were American Girl dolls, Sephora make-up, Betsie Johnson boutique trips, and Coach purses at four or five years old and a big sweet-sixteen party with all the trappings. All types of stereotypical girl stuff. When Gia came out to the family and laid out how they wanted to be seen and acknowledged by us, for a while, I was confused, taken back, and crying a lot. It was during Covid in 2020 when Gia told us they were going to begin hormone replacement and wanted to transition. My inner thoughts told me it had to do with what happened with Mike years ago or other things that we did that made Gia feel less important than our male-from-birth children. As time passed, we've all had time to digest and accept this reality. I've come to understand more and just accept that Gia is living their life in the way they are comfortable and happy. Honestly, I'm happy they are brave and strong enough to live the life that makes them feel whole. As long as they are working for good, being kind and honest with themselves and others, how can I be anything but proud of them and the life they are forging?

Life seems to be a constant trip on a merry-go-round. We keep going around and around each year. We do the same things in each season. We wait for time off and celebrate the same days. Most people look for consistency and feel safe when they know what to expect next.

What saved me was my work ethic and my deep desire to depend on no one. Not everyone can have that type of grit to get a job at ten, a paper route at eleven, and make a decision to do it for themselves at seventeen. The bottom line is, sacrifice for your kids and let them know you are happy to give them small things that show you support their education, such as books. A small gift, such as a book that you read with your child at night, will show them you care about them, want to spend time with them, and care about their journey to become a reader. A small act of kindness like this will plant the seeds for a positive life narrative in a young child's mind. Let your kids see you be kind by sacrificing your time and resources for them.

My life, my family, and the people that have come in for a season or a lifetime have all helped me grow and become the person I am today. Friends like Lisa and Roger and Kim and Ralph are friends that Anthony and I have made as adults, and these friendships, without the baggage of knowing me before my rewrite was underway, have been very special to me. They are all friends who would have been there back then, I know that, but it has been refreshing to have fresh eyes without the cloudiness of the past. They are friends who know us "after," who will listen and laugh about the past as you experienced it. With friends who only know you after your rewrite, you don't have to work as hard to prove or show them who you have become or how you want to be seen. Lifelong friends have their special place in accepting the entire story. They know how far you've come, but they will always see you as the person you have outgrown, because they were also part of it and had their own relationships and perspectives with the people involved.

During the first few months after Gia came out fully to the family, I was really lost and didn't understand how to go forward and shift my thinking about who Gia really was. I felt like they were lying to me all these years, and I didn't even know my own child. I felt like I was losing my daughter and that I had to bury her, take down all the pictures, and forget that I had a daughter – which was one of the only things I ever really wanted. I wanted a daughter, and Anthony promised me I'd have one, and when we found out I was pregnant with a girl, Anthony said, "I told you I'd give you a daughter." It was hard at first, and my friend Kim really extended herself, calling me and checking in to see how I was doing. Offering to meet for a cup of coffee to chat, she did her best to support me when she saw how difficult it was for me to accept at first. These are the tentpoles of a true friendship with people who will be there to hold you up when you are having a tough time doing it for yourself in difficult moments. I needed a little time to adjust and reorganize my thoughts, but I have accepted and grown with Gia. I'm very proud of who Gia is and understand that there are many people who need to dig down and find the courage to rewrite their narrative.

Many people I have been very close with have also rewritten their narratives. My husband, Anthony, is one. He ran a Mister Softee ice cream truck when I met and married him. Today he is a lead x-ray technician in a trauma center and an adjunct professor teaching x-ray at Essex County College. We have come far together, helping each other every step of the way. One pulling and one pushing at different times throughout our thirty-two years together. Without him, I would not be where I am today, that is for sure. He has saved me from the abyss more times than I'd like to admit. He was patient with me. I needed a few years to really work out all the baggage that I came to him with, but I know he believes I was worth the wait, and that's what keeps it a good fit all these years later.

Alex, my first husband, is another person who rewrote his narrative. He left the DJ business and party guy behind, went to college, and graduated with honors from St. Peter's University earning a degree in Theology. He is a Master Electrician and an involved Papou to our shared grandchildren. Without him, I wouldn't have learned many of the lessons that I needed to learn. He was a good teacher, for sure. He helped me find the courage inside myself to stand up and say, "Enough!"

When I was losing my mind at work, my friend Lisa showed me the way back to sanity. I will always remember how she held me up when I couldn't stand on my own. She helped me find my way to a much better position where I feel effective, which is important as a teacher. Teaching leaves you open to a lot of criticism. If you don't have a strong ego, solid self-esteem, and positive self-efficacy, you can easily be taken down. You have to continually reinforce yourself and practice mindfulness and wellness activities to keep yourself strong. If you don't take care of yourself, you can't take care of the young ones in front of you each day and have the patience and temperament to be who they really need you to be – kind, patient, and willing to make a personal connection. Share who you are, be relatable, and let them see that there is a way up and out because you have done it too. Always be humble with the children, not always with the adults. Let them teach you as you teach them. It's best when there's a reciprocal flow in the class where everyone feels at ease and comfortable enough to ask for help or to ask a question.

Two very important friends that I met early on in my rewrite are Jen S. and Jen L. We supported each other, talked, laughed, and grew into our professional lives together. We have shared so much that I would be remiss not to acknowledge their support during some of the toughest days of my professional and personal life. Helping me find my way forward with Gia after finding out about what Mike did, letting me cry on their shoulders when Alex ran away, or listening to me worry about Jake and his life's trajectory leading up to returning to college, and even being there when my marriage was falling apart. Figuring out and sharing life's problems together, and even now, after we have all flown off in different directions and don't work together any longer, we may not talk for a while, always knowing we are just a call away. True friends helped me hold it together each morning when things were unraveling. Suzanne, you too, we had a falling out, but the good outweighs the bad, and as you said to me recently, the laughs, we sure did laugh, my friend.

This is a chronicle of my journey to self-actualization, how I have come to understand my predestined purpose in this life, and what I believe I've been put here to accomplish, using my memories, experiences, and emotional knowledge to connect and present a way to own your past and make all the tears and heartache paid worth the price. Think of life as a thrift store and give everything you've been through a second chance to be useful going forward. If you can change the trajectory of someone's day and maybe their life because of something you can pull from your past that was negative and recycle it to help someone else, then you have the key to self-actualization.

It has been an honor and a therapeutic endeavor for me to mend my broken heart by exposing it to the students I've had through the years and by sharing my story through my testimony of unexplained events in my life, confessions, and a lens of owning who I've been and how the people in my life have helped me to find my calling and purpose. Healing myself and modeling how I was able to find my way. If someone told me when I was fifteen or sixteen that I would achieve the things I have, I would have laughed in their face and lit a cigarette.

Afterword:

"It's never too late to do the right thing."

- Nelson Mandela

This book has been simmering in my mind for many years. Knowing someone who wrote an honest memoir with a vision to make a positive difference truly inspired me. Lewis Spears modeled for me something that I wanted to accomplish. He put it in my reach because someone I knew did it. This is what helps children succeed in life. Having an up close example of success at something they have an interest in. Lewis Spears, the author of *"You're The Answer To The Problem: From the Hood to Harvard and Back Again."* reignited this idea in me that had been put to the side.

Even so, I was still unable to pull the trigger and get my ideas down on paper. After a very difficult year in 2022, I found myself in therapy for the first time. My therapist recommended Mel Robbins' book, *"The Five Second Rule."* If you have things that you want to get done, things that keep scratching at your back, but you just can't seem to quiet the itch, read this book. It will help you find your way by giving you a few brain exercises to employ. This guidebook helped me get this book out of my mind and on paper. I've always used the phrase "Just Do It" to push my students; pulling from the Nike motto and finally learning a strategy to scratch a little deeper helped me finally satisfy the itch. Thank you...Lewis Spears and Mel Robbins.

186

Thank you, Mom. I love you. You had a lot to deal with in your life, and until I was much older, I never really understood how little support you had when we were young. No one to leave us with to walk away for a breath. I couldn't look at things through your lens. I didn't understand the pain you lived with missing your best friend, your mother, and your other immediate family members all these years. In this life, I wish I had met my Grandma Dorothy, the angel in the closet. I know she must have been amazing, and one day we will have a cigarette together in the sky. We will let grandma cut the filters off of ours instead of taping filters to hers.

Without you, Anthony, over the past thirty-two years, being able to tell this story and feel that I have made it to self-actualization would have been impossible. You have been a true partner, supporting me and holding me up when I couldn't hold myself up and see my way through. Catching me when I was about to fall and never giving up on me. I love you, Ant. Thank you for our life, for raising Alex with me, and for bringing Jake and Gia to me as well. When it was too hard for me to hold on at times, you took both the reins and have always been a great role model for our family. I know it's safe to say, "We Made It!" We picked the perfect wedding song all those years ago. We couldn't have known how apropos it would always be.

"You fill my heart with gladness, take away all my sadness, ease my troubles, that's what you do." - Rod Stewart, *"Have I Told You Lately"*

Printed in the USA
CPSIA information can be obtained
at www.ICGtesting.com
CBHW081027100624
9827CB00014B/166